THE YEAR

THE COBBLER

Reflections on a lifetime and a season supporting Northampton Town FC

Edited by Rodney Marshall
Foreword by Peter Gleasure

Having followed Northampton Town FC for over forty years, I want to thank everyone who has shaped or coloured the journey. In particular, my father, Roger, for sowing the Cobblers seed on a wet, windy Saturday back in October 1975 – he wouldn't have done it had he known where it would lead; my brother, Chris, for joining me on some of the long away trips in the wilderness years of the early 1980s; Peter, Sharon and Eileen Gleasure for their car lifts, kindness and friendship; Martyn Ingram for driving me to the likes of Edgar Street, Turf Moor, Vale Park, Spotland... as enthusiastic a fan as you'll find; editor Rob Marshall (no relation) for encouraging me to write for the fanzine, WALOC; and Judith and Tomas, for sharing the famine (and feast) in more recent years.

My thanks go to Cobblers legend Peter Gleasure for the Foreword and to Jeremy Casey at the *Chronicle & Echo* for the front cover photo which was taken by © Kirsty Edmonds.

This book is dedicated to the memory of all the heroes – sung or unsung – of Northampton Town, throughout its one hundred and nineteen year history, including AJ 'Pat' Darnell, Herbert Chapman, Edwin Lloyd Davies, Dave Bowen, Cliff Holton, Jack English, Tommy Fowler and Brian Lomax.

"I'm at it, I'm at it, I'm exhausted...Let's get the bleeding deal done."
(Chris Wilder, BBC Radio Northampton interview, 21/11/2015)

'Forget Leicester – Northampton Town are English football's story of the season.'
(*The Sun*, 25/03/2016)

'Northampton are obdurate...they win games that they should draw and they draw games they should lose. Wilder has done a remarkable job...be sure to keep an eye on that man.'
(Rod Liddle, *The Sunday Times*, 01/05/2016)

'From exhausting to enthralling. That just about sums up this season.'
(Joe Townsend, BBC Radio Northampton)

'It's a great story. It's a story we wish we'd all never had to go through, but it has come out the right way...in a happy ending and you like to think, at times, that the good guys win.'
(Chris Wilder, NTFC website 26/04/2016)

'If someone wrote a book about this season, you'd never believe it was true.'
(Marc Richards, NTFC website 31/05/2016)

CONTENTS

FOREWORD

by Peter Gleasure

'The fans have to take a lot of the praise as well: never giving up hope, they are an absolute credit to the club and can hold their heads up high. And that is what a club is all about: the fans.'

Is it really almost thirty years since we were champions, winning the old Fourth Division title? It doesn't seem that long ago. Graham Carr came in at Easter 1985 when we were bottom of the Football League, back in the days of re-election. He instilled what we were missing — confidence. He was hard, but fair. If he didn't think you were pulling your weight he told you in no uncertain terms, but any tough words were forgotten the following day. His greatest strength was his ability to motivate everyone. He brought in players like Richard Hill and Trevor Morley who had started at professional clubs but been discarded. He knew they were quality footballers and offered them a second bite of the cherry, knowing they would be determined to succeed second time around. Fitness, work rate and desire were important to him.

He and Clive Walker made a good team, it was a great combination; but it was never a case of 'good cop, bad cop'. Most of the coaching was down to Clive, while Graham used his knowledge to bring in top players. I remember telling some lads on a stag weekend, before the title season began, that I was confident we could go up, that it was worth putting some money on us to win the league. Before long, family and friends were choosing Northampton Town on their pools coupon each week, bankers to win. Occasionally you have those seasons where everything clicks into place and a run of wins brings such belief.

The following season (in the old Third Division), only a year after the play-offs were created, we nearly made it into them, losing at Sunderland in our final match. However, the team was already breaking up. When players perform well, they get scouted, and it is inevitable that they are sold to bigger clubs. Morley, Hill and McGoldrick all went on to play at the very top. Just a few years later we were back in the Fourth Division and the new chairman was cutting every possible corner. We would return from training to find no hot water for the showers; he'd turned the gas off. Pre-match meals were replaced by sandwiches and tea and coffee flasks at a motorway service station. It was back to the bad old days, only worse. Having wasted eighteen months when the manager (Theo Foley) discarded me after a defensive mix-up against Peterborough, the club went into administration. [1] I had hoped, with eighteen months left on a new three year contract, to take my coaching badges and maybe go into that side of the game. But that's football. It is a great shame that my time at Northampton ended that way but I had eight fantastic years at the club before then, lots of happy memories and the fans were always very good to me.

We reached 99 points in the 1986-87 season, and so did the 2015-16 side, but I actually think that the current team's achievement is greater. To win the title with everything that was going on away from the pitch – and the club so close to going under – is fantastic. The fans have to take a lot of the praise as well: never giving up hope, they are an absolute credit to the club and can hold their heads up high. And that is what a club is all about: the fans.

© Peter Gleasure
June 2nd 2016

1. Ten senior players were sacked, including Peter.

Peter Gleasure is the third highest appearance maker for Northampton Town in the club's history. A former player of the season, he runs his own driving school in Luton. (It seemed fitting to have a Foreword provided by someone who was part of the side the last time the Cobblers were Champions.)

NORTHAMPTON TOWN FC TIMELINE

1897 Northampton Town Football Club formed

1901-02 Joined the Southern League

1907 Return of Herbert Chapman as player-manager

1908-09 Southern League Champions, under Chapman

1909 Charity Shield runners-up

1920-21 Joined the Football League

1932-33 Holland national team beaten 4-0 during a club tour

1933-34 First Division leaders Huddersfield beaten away in FA Cup

1957-58 Arsenal beaten 3-1 in the FA Cup

1959 Return of Dave Bowen as player-manager

1960-61 Promoted from Division Four for the first time, under Bowen

1962-63 Third Division Champions, under Bowen

1964-65 Second Division runners-up, under Bowen

1965-66 'Season in the Sun' – top flight for the only time in club's history

1966 Highest ever League attendance of 24, 523 versus Fulham

1969 Back in the Football League basement

1969-70 George Best scores six in 8-2 FA Cup home defeat by Manchester United

1984-85 Lowest ever League attendance of 942 versus Chester City

1986-87 Fourth Division Champions, under Graham Carr

1992 Administration; Formation of Supporters Trust

1993-94 Finished bottom of the Football League for the only time in club's history

1994 Move from the County Ground to newly-built Sixfields Stadium

1996-97 Swansea beaten 1-0 in play-off final at Wembley in centenary year

1997-98 Lost 1-0 to Grimsby in play-off final at Wembley

2010-11 Liverpool beaten at Anfield in League Cup after penalty shoot-out

2012-13 Lost 3-0 to Bradford City in play-off final at Wembley

2015-16 Champions of League 2, shattering a host of club records

2015-16 RECORD BREAKERS

10 Northampton Town club (League) records broken/equalled during the season:

- Unbeaten run (24)
- Unbeaten away run (16)
- Consecutive wins (10)
- Consecutive away wins (8)
- Away victories (14)
- Fewest defeats (5)
- Fewest away defeats (2)
- League points (99)
- Manager of the Month awards (3)
- Players selected for the PFA divisional side (3)

NORTHAMPTON TOWN FC TIMELINE 2015-16

May 2015 Buckingham Group suspend work on East Stand due to 'non-payment'

24/06/2015 David Cardoza announces takeover talks with Indian consortium

06/08/2015 Teenage striker Ivan Toney sold to Newcastle for 'undisclosed fee'

12/09/2015 Fan demonstration – '#We Want Answers' – at Oxford match

25/09/2015 Borough Council gives NTFC three weeks to pay £10.25 million loan

12/10/2015 London-based Indian takeover collapses

15/10/2015 HMRC launches winding-up petition over unpaid tax bill

21/10/2015 Buckingham release statement concluding 'gross mismanagement and /or misappropriation of a very significant public loan'

01/11/2015 Cobblers Supporters Trust pioneer Brian Lomax passes away

06/11/2015 *Guardian* newspaper investigation: 'Scandal of Missing Millions'

16/11/2015 High Court winding-up petition hearing adjourned for two weeks

21/11/2015 Chris Wilder makes rousing takeover speech at Meadow Lane

23/11/2015 Police serve warrant and remove files and computers from Sixfields

26/11/2015 Kelvin Thomas completes takeover

27/11/2015 Insolvency hearing adjourned

10/12/2015 Insolvency proceedings withdrawn by Borough Council

11/12/2015 Wilder named November Sky Bet League 2 Manager of the Month

12/12/2016 Cobblers top of League 2 after 4-3 win at Luton

19/01/2016 7,040 Cobblers fans travel away to Milton Keynes in the FA Cup

09/02/2016 Wilder named January Sky Bet League 2 Manager of the Month

13/02/2016 Biggest win of the season recorded at Leyton Orient

16/02/2016 University of Northampton extend shirt sponsorship/partnership

23/02/2016 Victory at York makes it ten consecutive wins in League 2

25/02/2016 Work restarts on East Stand

11/03/2016 Wilder named February Sky Bet League 2 Manager of the Month

25/03/2016 Media attention on NTFC during international break; *The Sun*: 'Forget Leicester – Northampton Town are English football's story of the season.'

02/04/2016 Lower tier of East Stand opens with 1,924 new seats

09/04/2016 Record Sixfields crowd (7579) sees promotion confirmed

16/04/2016 League 2 title sealed at Exeter City

17/04/2016 Wilder named Manager of the Year at the Football League Awards; Adam Smith named Goalkeeper of the Year

21/04/2016 Smith, O'Toole and Holmes named in PFA divisional side

22/04/2016 Nike announced as new official kit partners

30/04/2016 New record Sixfields crowd (7664) sees NTFC receive League 2 trophy

01/05/2016 Awards dinner at the County Ground, the club's spiritual home

07/05/2016 Season concludes with win at Fratton Park, extending unbeaten league run to 24 matches

08/05/2016 Open-top bus parade with thousands lining the streets and the market square; civic reception at the Guildhall

09/05/2016 Chris Wilder and Alan Knill open talks with Charlton Athletic

11/05/2016 Talks break down between Wilder/Knill and Charlton

12/05/2016 Wilder and Knill sign for Sheffield United

19/05/2016 Former Wales international and Port Vale boss Rob Page appointed as Cobblers manager on a three year contract

PREFACE:
SINS OF THE FATHER

by Rodney Marshall

'A lifetime supporting a club such as Northampton Town is a labour of love.'

How many of us blame our fathers for introducing us to the football club which we became destined to follow for the rest of our lives? In my case, it wasn't even my local club. Born in Leicester, my father was brought up in Northampton at a time when the shoe manufacturing industry still thrived in this East Midland town. My grandfather was a salesman and later a branch director of a now defunct shoe company, Norvic. After National Service, studying English at Cambridge University and playing some cricket for Northamptonshire seconds, my father moved to London to pursue a career as a television and film scriptwriter. Having grown up as a Cobblers fan, the sixties roller coaster of fourth tier to first and back again had left him disenchanted and he began to follow Bobby Robson's Ipswich Town as I grew up in South London. However, he made a fateful mistake one autumn day in 1975. We were staying at my grandparents in Spinney Hill, Northampton. It was a miserable Saturday morning, the lashing rain guaranteeing a day stuck inside. Lying on the carpet reading the sports pages of *The Daily Telegraph* he looked up and announced, "I don't know about everybody else, but I'm off to the Cobblers." It was the first season since those heady days of the mid-sixties – when Northampton had briefly rubbed shoulders with Liverpool, Everton, Tottenham, Arsenal, Manchester United et al – when the club was threatening to win promotion and they had a local derby with Watford. Three generations of the Marshall family watched a 3-0 win and something was born inside me.

Probably realising the error of his ways, my father would take us to more glamorous venues in subsequent years, watching top flight football at Loftus Road, Highbury, Stamford Bridge, Upton Park and Portman Road. I even had a brief fling with Wolverhampton Wanderers as I liked their black and gold kit. However, my father had sown a seed and each time I visited my grandparents I asked to be taken to the County Ground, the strangest of football grounds. The Edwardian brick façade and maroon corrugated signage gave the impression of a perfectly normal lower league venue. Nevertheless, as soon as you entered you were immediately reminded of the warning not to judge a book by its cover. It was a cricket ground, with football stands added to two and a half sides.

Opposite the main stand was nothing, except for an unrestricted view of the cricket pitch, the scoreboard, cricket stands, nets and the pavilion. The open away end didn't even extend beyond the goal as a bowling green club took up the remaining space. I always liked it, though. Never mind that the hallowed football turf became a cricket car park in the summer months. It meant that I could watch cricket matches from the empty terraces during summer holidays, daydreaming about the football season to come. It was quirky and different, perfect for a fan of Northampton Town. Well, a perfect fit for me anyway.

At our all-boys London junior school, most pupils followed a team: Chelsea, QPR, Arsenal, Tottenham, Leeds, Liverpool or Manchester United. Supporting the Cobblers simply led to bemused questions, such as "What league are they in?" "Why don't you support a proper club?" These questions have been repeated throughout my lifetime, by family, friends, colleagues or complete strangers.

In those formative years I missed out on the glamour of big matches, national media and television coverage, local respect in the playground. The advantages were seemingly modest, but ones which I nevertheless cherished: in that now vanished age of letter writing – rather than tweeting – my nervous, star-struck attempts at fan-mail were *always* answered by players: politely, enthusiastically and often with a home address and telephone number attached in case I wanted to talk Cobblers with them; many of the players knew me by name and face; complimentary away tickets would be thrust into my hands after long treks to the unglamorous outposts of Division Four: Crewe, Chester, Hartlepool, Darlington or Tranmere. [1] I sensed that my presence genuinely mattered during the bleak early to mid-1980s years when home attendances hovered alarmingly above the 1,000 mark and, on one infamous occasion, dipped below.

I should confess that, like a worn-out drug addict, I have tried to quit many times, even moving country for a number of years to remove myself from temptation. However, it hasn't worked. The sins of the father have cursed the son, and been passed on now to my own boy, Tomas.

Supporting the Cobblers recalls the lyrics from Frank Sinatra's classic song *My Way*: I've travelled each and every highway. I've had my regrets. I've loved, I've laughed and cried. I've had more than my share of losing. Seasons of mid-table mediocrity or relegation roulette dogfights are expected and endured with a battle-hardened fidelity. However, all of this suffering has simply made the rare successes sweeter; surreal in the case of the 2015-16 season. A lifetime of supporting a club such as Northampton Town is – like this book – a labour of love.

© Rodney Marshall
Suffolk, UK,
June 2016

1. One of those players, goalkeeper Peter Gleasure, became a life-long friend. More than thirty years on from our first meeting, Peter and I made the trip to Kenilworth Road together last December, before supporting our respective teams from opposing ends of the ground. It is hard to imagine something similar occurring with a top-flight player.

INTRODUCTION

The Year of the Cobbler is a book published to celebrate and reflect upon the 2015-16 football season, a truly magnificent one for everyone connected with Northampton Town FC. However, it also allows individual writers to explore their lifelong connections with football in general and the Cobblers in particular, the club we follow home and away. Usually this is more out of hope than expectation. However, just occasionally you get one of those seasons which dreams are made of...

Gareth Willsher – Head of Media at Northampton Town – offers his personal inside view of what the first few months of last season were like off the pitch. From attempting to soldier on ('business as usual') to the difficulties which arise when you're not being paid – 'Things were difficult at home, Christmas was six or seven weeks away, money was running out but we somehow kept things ticking' – to the realisation that a more militant approach was needed: 'We were dangerous, we were unpaid, angry staff with public sympathy, the inside view from the club and the ear of the media.' Ultimately, the staff and the club's future was secured, and Willsher praises the supporters for the multiple roles they played: demonstrating the potential of the club to the chairman-in-waiting; encouraging staff and players with the sheer size of both their passion and turnouts. It is a strange tale: on the one hand, a heart-warming story of solidarity, a united effort; on the other, a chilling, startlingly sober one which we should carefully digest before reading on.

Racing Post sports editor **Phil Agius** – like many Northampton fans – finds that 'Cobblers matches sit like milestones along the major events of my life'. Here he reviews the season through 'ten games I went to that most captured the essence of the Cobblers'. They are not so much mini-match reports, more a way of structuring both his general thoughts about our club and the wonderful unpredictability of football, as a remarkable campaign unfolded.

Jefferson Lake covered the club for the *Chronicle & Echo*, a post he held for more than a decade before leaving for *Sky Sports*. Here he reflects on a vital ingredient for success which – in the world of professional football – is almost as rare as rocking horse poo: namely, patience. With fans calling for manager Chris Wilder's dismissal in the final days of 2014, it seemed all too likely that yet another Northampton manager would bite the Sixfields dust. Thankfully, the then chairman gave him another transfer window to turn things around. As Lake reflects, 'Maybe we could all do with being a bit more patient. With football, with our relationships, with our lives.'

Freelance writer **Rodney Marshall** explores how his support for the Cobblers spiralled out of control, developing from a harmless hobby into an obsession which threatened to shape and control everything: school life, career choices, even romantic encounters. He examines how technology has changed our collective and individual experience as football fans. He also reflects on the 'shared surrealism' of the 2015-16 season – 'people had suffered collectively and now the joy was communal' – and highlights some of the future challenges facing our beloved club. Looking ahead to the new season, he goes off-thread in search of a genuine local rival for Northampton Town. In an appendix at the back of the book, he describes his encounter with the lower-league club Chamois Niortais, uncovering a potential French twin for the Cobblers.

BBC Sport journalist **Tom Rostance** offers a refreshing honesty in his article. After a lengthy period of failure, we need our perennially underachieving club to provide us with a memorable campaign in order to remind us why we follow our team through all those wilderness years. 'You can say what you like about sport being about taking part but the cold, hard facts are that nothing beats winning every week. And this was the season when we Cobblers fans finally got a chance to savour that.' We inwardly crave both that injection of excitement and the restoration of a sense of pride, even if we stoically avow that we will remain loyal however bad it gets. A glorious season of success reinvigorates all of us.

Seasoned Cobblers fan **Norman Maycock** takes us back to the glory, glory years of the early 1960s, but also examines the decisions a young football fan has to make when s/he starts supporting a club in a period of famine: to stick with it, 'pecking at crumbs on the way', 'or move on to other things'. Maycock chose to stick, and his high-octane, humorous, stream-of-consciousness narrative contains plenty of truths about football and life itself, including 'man's eternal conflict between pie and profundity'.

Lifelong Cobblers fan and *Chronicle & Echo* Chief Sports Writer **Jeremy Casey** – in common with many Northampton fans – takes a pragmatic approach to manager Chris Wilder's departure. His article pays homage to a man who took the club from the bottom to the summit of the Football League's basement division. He reflects that this is simply the end of an exciting chapter, hoping, like all of us, that the next instalment is also enthralling. From his journalist point-of-view he acknowledges that this 'was the season that just kept on giving, with story after story after story coming out of the club. So much so, that at times it was hard to keep up!'

For *BBC Radio Northampton* reporter **Joe Townsend** this will go down as a memorable first season following the Cobblers, one he is unlikely to forget whatever he goes on to achieve in his broadcasting career. Here he reflects on his baptism of fire. Interviewing Chris Wilder was rarely straightforward and, unsurprisingly, Townsend highlights the manager's post-match 'impassioned pitch-side rant' at Meadow Lane as a key moment in the journalist's debut campaign: 'Trust me, it was more soliloquy than interview. I tentatively held out that microphone, just far enough away to feel safe...Well, safeish.' (Townsend's article is an extended version of the piece which appeared on the BBC website when the Cobblers had secured promotion.)

Martyn Ingram is another seasoned fan who begins his story in the 1960s. He reflects upon the fact that heroes are created in our minds when we are young, impressionable and more imaginative, when we naively believe that playing for Northampton Town should represent the peak of any player's career. As we get older, realism sets in, but the true fan never becomes overtly cynical. We retain a child-like belief and still harbour hope. His purchase – as a fully-formed adult – of a Hotel End turnstile illustrates the lengths we will go to in maintaining that magical dreamland which was created by that very first game. He also examines how the culture of the game has changed, both on the pitch and off it.

Fairy tale season? Or cautionary tale? Journalist **Tom Reed**'s article reminds us that the magnificent 2015-16 campaign on the pitch was matched by an equally dark story off it, one which 'may get worse when the true details come to light.' The season may have ended, but the quest to retrieve the 'missing millions' (of public funds) continues. He widens his field of inquiry to question how professional football clubs are run in the light of 'the dysfunctional club ownership model in England'.

James Heneghan reflects on his first campaign as the *Chronicle & Echo*'s matchday reporter for Northampton Town. He explores all the ingredients which combined to create such a memorable season: off-field adversity; the unwavering support of the fans; the arrival of a saviour; an exhilarating style of attacking football; the high energy, relentless pressing; and the never-say-die mind-set of Wilder's team. As he reminds us, the final league table only tells half the story; few of the wins were comfortable ones. Perhaps what impressed Heneghan most was the unity: 'Northampton fans and staff didn't just save their club, they came together to inspire one of the most remarkable rags-to-riches stories ever witnessed. Football needs more stories like Northampton's, proof that the bad guys don't always win and that there's always hope, always another day.'

Tom Ingram explores what it feels like to grow up supporting a lower league side which is not even your local one. He also speculates on what he might have done had Northampton Town FC actually folded. The possibility forced all of us, I would imagine, to pose similar questions about the nature of our support or devotion, and what it would mean to lose our club. (His article arrived as the deadline passed, hence why this piece is situated in the extra time section, or the back row.)

There is, naturally, 'connective tissue' binding the various articles. Together they tell a story about our need for roots, heroes, hope, patience, excitement and solidarity, including the sense of a communal, shared identity and purpose. In our ever-increasingly virtual world, this real passion is, arguably, more important than ever before.

While *The Year of the Cobbler* draws on both journalists and ordinary supporters' experiences over a lifetime of following both 'the beautiful game' in general and our football club in particular, the focus is also on a unique season in which increasing fear that NTFC might have played its last game gave way to something unexpectedly positive and increasingly incredible. All played out against the backdrop of an unfinished concrete block which seemed to represent both the failures and follies of the past *and* also the (forlorn?) hope of future fulfilment. The week in which spring arrived, and promotion was almost within touching distance, shiny new seats were installed in the lower tier of the controversial East Stand. Like colourful flowers blooming in a previously barren wilderness, the act seemed like a symbolic one.

UNITED EFFORT

by Gareth Willsher

'We were dangerous, we were unpaid, angry staff with public sympathy, the inside view from the club and the ear of the media.'

When Rodney asked me to write some thoughts on the 2015/16 season, it was hard to know where to begin. I must stress that these are my own personal thoughts and recollections, and are not to be taken as an official view of the club.

Amazing, unbelievable, once in a lifetime are all accurate descriptions of what happened, but of course while the season had the perfect ending of promotion and then the League 2 title, there was a lot of drama that we survived before Marc Richards lifted that trophy high into the air at Sixfields at around 5pm on Saturday April 30th.

I guess the best place to start is at the beginning. It was on Wednesday June 24th 2015 at 2pm that Chairman David Cardoza announced his intention to sell the club. Of course, in my role I had some advanced notice of this and had prepared the announcement, but not a lot. It had come out of the blue for the staff as much as supporters. Of course we knew the East Stand work had stopped and we had no idea when it would start again, but this sudden announcement meant things changed quickly.

The job of all staff was simply to get on with things in a 'business as usual' way as the Chairman continued in discussions to sell the club. These discussions took place away from the club. We had no idea whether the deal would be done in a few weeks or longer, but we just had to get on with things.

Pre-season began but we knew that things would be a struggle when the club really battled to pay the June wages. They were paid in the end, but some were late. In particular we felt for Chris Wilder and Alan Knill. They had sold the idea of joining the club to the likes of David Buchanan and Nicky Adams on the basis that it was a stable club, a solid club, and at the end of their first month there was a battle to pay the wages.

The cash-flow issues settled down temporarily with the sale of Ivan Toney and the Capital One Cup tie at Newcastle United, and that allowed a temporary return to 'normal'. The season began but by mid-September, with no real update or progress on the sale of the club, the supporters ran a 'We want answers' campaign at the Oxford United game. At the same time, the Borough Council set a deadline of three weeks for the repayment of their £10.25m loan.

Unquestionably the sale of the club was drifting, and while many of us felt helpless to try and move things along, the date set by the council at least meant a process began that would eventually lead to a deadline, and we knew that would, in turn, eventually bring things to a head. However, at this time, we simply carried on as normal. We had our day to day jobs to do, and the Chairman was dealing with the other issues.

With the 'We want answers' campaign running, we had to stress to supporters that we really didn't know any more than was in the public domain. We weren't in possession of any more information, so we just had to keep going, keep doing the day to day jobs and allow matters to take their course.

By the time we got to October, we were thinking, without any inside information, that every time we got to a Monday that this would be the week things would be resolved. We knew the money that paid the wages in August and September had run out, and with each passing day it was getting harder and harder for CEO James Whiting to pay the bills in any form of normal way. The club was struggling to pay suppliers, rumours were spreading and we had no idea how, or if, we would be paid at the end of October. The HMRC court date was set, the bank account was frozen and that made it hard for James to keep things ticking.

James and I attended an open meeting of supporters at the Guildhall during October. It was a tough meeting to attend: we had very few answers to the key questions but we knew the only way the club would come through this would be a joint, united effort from everyone who cared and it was crucial we were there to try and shed some light on the situation we found ourselves in. That said, I go back to the earlier point, we didn't know of any more information than was in the public domain.

By this point, despite our best efforts, the situation was on the slide. We were still trying to keep things on an even keel, but it was getting harder and harder. I often wonder, with the benefit of hindsight, if we should have tried to bring things to a head earlier, but at the time we were just trying to keep things steady, to support the players and to keep the club in the best shape possible for the new owners.

As October went on, it became clear we weren't going to be paid. It didn't come as a bolt out of the blue, more a gradual confirmation that we worked out ourselves as we weren't being told anything. Payday was due on Friday October 30th, the day before we played away at Newport County, but we had resigned ourselves to our pay not appearing a few days before that.

Things were now escalating quickly, but the impending court dates actually gave us some sort of end date. Yes it was a risk, the courts could put us into administration and all the pain that would bring, but we at least knew that would bring a resolution, one way or another.

The next week we were at Coventry City in the FA Cup, in front of that huge, fantastic away support. We were no closer to knowing if or when we would get paid, but those court dates gave us some form of timescale. Things were difficult at home, Christmas was six or seven weeks away, money was running out but we somehow kept things ticking. The turnout of support at Coventry that day was fantastic, and it was the sheer numbers travelling, as well as the passion showed, that gave real encouragement to the staff and players. Writing in the Luton programme, Kelvin Thomas also said the level of support that afternoon impressed him, and proved to him the potential the club has.

'Keeping things ticking' remained the case for a couple of weeks, at least until the build up to the Notts County game. We knew we were approaching crunch time, the administration hearing was only a week or so away, and the concern now was time. We had felt for many weeks that each passing week would be the week where things got resolved, but here we were, a few days before the Notts County game, still none the wiser. This was when the staff, as a group, were close to taking action. We visited the Sixfields Tavern for lunch on Thursday November 19th, kindly paid for by the Sixfields Travel Club, and we were at the end of our tether. It wasn't so much the situation that was getting to us, it was the lack of progress, the lack of updates. Kelvin Thomas had made a public statement to say that he and his colleagues were ready and waiting, but were thinking of pulling out due to that lack of progress. Some of us at the lunch were keen to not work on the Friday, to use the publicity of a 'strike' to try and put pressure on David Cardoza to sell, but others felt we should keep going. In the end, we decided to keep going, our main concern was continuing to support Chris Wilder, Alan Knill and the players, who by now were making excellent progress up the table. We didn't want to harm their pre-match plans.

We did, however, realise that we were in the end game and while we continued to work, we knew this was the time to exert more pressure. Our communication strategy until now had been to keep things stable, steady and 'business as usual.' Now, we felt it was time to change that. We were dangerous, we were unpaid, angry staff with public sympathy, the inside view from the club and the ear of the media. I went in to BBC Radio Northampton on Friday Night Sport the night before the Notts County game to encourage David Cardoza to sell the club. That was the start of a busy weekend but the real explosion came the following day.

I spoke with James Whiting on the morning of the Notts County game and he said that Chris Wilder also felt that this was the time to go public and that he might have his say to the media after the Notts game. We agreed that this was the right time; it was now or never. I was praying, more than ever, that we won at Notts County. We wanted a win so it gave Chris a platform to talk about the off-the-field stuff. Had we lost he would have had to field questions about a defeat but the way we played (and won) meant he didn't have to. At the final whistle I made my way down to the dressing room, as is usual, and waited outside for Chris to finish his post-match debrief with the players. Usually he would come out and we would briefly discuss which players would speak to the media but on this occasion I thought it would be best to remind him that we felt it was time to have his say. The door burst open and before I could even say anything he responded with 'Doing it,' and didn't break stride. I knew then he was in the mood to say his piece.

BBC Radio Northampton's Joe Townsend took a few minutes to get down to pitch side and in those minutes Chris was pacing, bristling. The minute the microphone was turned on, Chris just went for it. The interview itself is now legendary, and I am sure it played a huge part in selling the club. I had pre-warned Elliot Stonhill, our media assistant who was working back in Northampton as he often does on away matchdays, to be prepared for it and so we were ready to react and publish the comments as quickly as possible.

The reaction was huge. Making our way home from Meadow Lane that night, I decided to follow that up with a *Facebook* post on the club account, coupled with some historic images from the club's past, appealing to the Chairman to sell the club. It was all part of the plan to support Chris's comments.

The rest of that weekend was busy. There were plenty of phone calls flying around on the Saturday evening and Sunday until, finally, that Sunday evening, we believed privately that the sale of the club to Kelvin Thomas and his colleagues was agreed.

We now know that wasn't the end of the saga, we know there were still plenty of hurdles for Kelvin to overcome, but by the Thursday of that week, the deal had gone through and we could begin to move forward.

And that really was that. We quickly went back to being a 'normal' football club, we just got on with our jobs and the players just kept getting better and better. Kelvin got everyone together on his first day to say it was important not to relax, to put the energy we had invested in keeping the club in some sort of shape into pushing forward, and the season just got better and better.

Others will no doubt describe the fantastic performances since then, and to have lost only one game since mid-October is simply sensational. Full credit to the players, they deserve all the celebrations, all the praise and the memories of the 2015/16 season will live on. For many of the staff, we simply went back to doing our 'normal' jobs, but this time with the backdrop of a club making progress rather than battling for survival.

© Gareth Willsher

MEMORIES
&
MILESTONES
by Phil Agius

'Cobblers matches sit like milestones along the major events of my life'.

One of the most satisfying aspects of the unforgettable 2015-16 season is that for large parts of it the Cobblers were still the Cobblers. Even while winning the league by 13 points, we managed to fit in a frustratingly slow start and a financial crisis. Even since wrapping it up we've had football's Grinches telling us the team beaten out of sight in second were a better side, a manager change and angst about our best players potentially leaving – all comfortably familiar.

I've seen a lot of NTFC teams come and go since my dad first hoisted me onto the wooden platform that ran along the concrete wall at the front of the old County Ground main stand as a six-year old. Derrick Christie was the fastest thing I'd ever seen. I couldn't believe the speed as he whizzed past hoping to deliver a cross for the head of big George Reilly.

Memories of the 1986-87 – and I am not happy with my brain for this - mostly seem to consist of hoping we wouldn't score too many because as a timid teenager I wasn't a massive fan of the surge down the Hotel End which a Richard Hill special would spark. What would we have thought if someone had told us then that we'd have to wait 29 years for another title-winning season?

Cobblers matches sit like milestones along the major events of my life. I remember telling my boss on my first day at work: "My team lost 5-2 at home on Saturday (Halifax, September 1992). I saw his mind whirring, mentally crossing off the top-flight teams who had not lost 5-2 in his head before he said: "Who's that then?" "Northampton," I said and we were off on the right foot – he was a Brentford fan and we knew we would understand each other. That was just three weeks after one of my all-time favourite Cobblers games – the 1-1 draw against Hereford where they had four men sent off – equalised with nine men and the ref spent so long dismissing their players we barely had a chance to get a winner.

That was proper Cobblers, and the flops, failures and frustrations are all going to come around more times on the wheel of fortune than the glory seasons, so we must make the most of them when we hit the jackpot.

The Atkins Wembley trips were great – Roy Hunter and Ray Warburton both make my all-time Cobblers XI – but nothing has ever topped survival at Shrewsbury at the end of that same 1992-93 season as a fan experience. That is what it is all about. Some of us still dream of a team of Phil Chards and the chant of "Ooh, aah, Gavin's arse" was much more witty and original than the more famous Eric Cantona version.

Work, family commitments and living 100 miles away from town mean I can't go to every game but to tell the story of this amazing season, I've picked out ten games I went to that most captured the essence of the Cobblers.

August 18: Barnet away, Lost 2-0

If you've made an impressive start to the season there's a sure-fire way of putting a dampener on things – let me attend. The Cobblers had won their first three games – against Bristol Rovers, Blackpool and Exeter – when my schedule allowed me to see the class of 2015-16 for the first time at Barnet's low-key new home The Hive.

My first sight of the champions led me to do something I had never done before at a Cobblers game – leave before the end.

The game had very few clues that we were watching potential champions. Chris Wilder had tinkered with the line-up – not on the scale of Aidy Boothroyd's mystifying Bradford selection but it was arguably too early to be resting Marc Richards (he's forgiven 100 times over now but still...). Ricky Holmes injured himself in the warm-up, not to be seen again until December, Jason Taylor was sent off conceding the penalty from which we went 1-0 down to a team on zero points, and the defence was frankly a shambles with Josh Lelan and Rod McDonald looking hopelessly out of their depth. We were clearly a more talented side but were hit by a succession of sucker punches and when John Akinde scored his second in added time I headed for the exits. Classic Cobblers. This is going to be our year? Yeah, right.

September 5: Dagenham home, Lost 2-1

Another episode of old-school Cobblers clowning. Having lost to Barnet, Town managed to hand another team their first win of the season, this time on a plate. Five minutes after going ahead with a Marc Richards header, we concede a breakaway equaliser, then a collision between McDonald and Adam Smith gifts Dagenham their first victory over Northampton in 11 attempts. Dagenham of all teams. Even in the greatest of seasons, you can rely on the Cobblers to let you down in new and exciting ways …

September 26: Orient home, Drew 1-1

Anyone who did the sensible thing and left before the end would have remembered one of the most boring games of the season. Anyone who stayed until the end had their heart lifted into the heavens by an added-time 'winner' from Dominic Calvert-Lewin and then saw those claret hearts smashed on the rocks of a Dean Cox free kick that arrowed into the top left corner. I know there was nothing Adam Smith could do about it – the flight was directly in line with my seat in the Lower West and it was going in from the second it left his foot, probably before. And it was never a free kick either. Cross unjust last-minute equaliser conceded off your bingo card.

November 24: Crawley away, Won 2-1

Sharper-eyed readers will have spotted that in chronicling an amazing season of success, we have so far revisited two poor defeats and a frustrating draw. The first win on the list did not come until November, in the game that's closest to home for me.

Born in the Barratt and raised in Kingsthorpe, my career took me to Crawley in 1995 and I've been here ever since. I met my wife Jo when she was the press officer for Crawley Town and in the years that followed, when they were a non-league side with ambitions no greater than reaching the Conference, I helped out with that and wrote for the programme.

It was in that capacity that I first came across an impressive young manager called Chris Wilder at Crawley's Broadfield Stadium in what *Wikipedia* tells me must have been 2005 or 2006. The man who would shape the Cobblers' title-winning side stood out among a fairly mixed bag of opposing managers in the post-match press conferences. He had done a tremendous job on a small budget getting part-time Halifax into play-off contention, spoke well and came over as someone with purpose and vision. When the focused and polite guy in the blue Conference anorak was lured away from Oxford almost a decade later to don a claret tie I was delighted. That, of course, was no guarantee of success – I'd also thought Gary Johnson would do a good job.

Back in 2015-16, Wilder returned to the Broadfield as manager of a club on the brink of having a future again. Kelvin Thomas's takeover was due to be confirmed any day and there was an air of optimism in the away stand.

There were, of course, more typical Cobblers moments, a sending-off (Brendan Moloney this time) and a penalty that was initially saved, but there were other, more unusual happenings too, such as the penalty rebound being converted by Joel Byrom, John-Joe O'Toole spanking a left-footed shot in from 25 yards and us winning with ten men. It could have been 5-0 with 11. This was strange.

December 28: Accrington home, Won 1-0

The Cobblers are a family and the Cobblers are about family. My great-grandad Percy Thorneycroft was a Supporters Club official before I was born, my dad took me to my first games – I remember him telling me I 'looked like Paul Stratford' when I had my shirt untucked. I also remember him informing me the Cobblers had signed Mario Kempes for £4m after the 1978 World Cup – it sounds plausible when you're seven, okay?

Dad and I were at Sixfields together 36 years later when we beat Oxford on the last day to stay up – not quite as dramatic as Shrewsbury, but it was iffy before John Marquis – who can surely claim to be the club's best loan signing ever for his two important contributions – equalised.

It's unlikely I'd see my cousins Neil and Darren Chapman half as often if the Cobblers didn't exist, but it's always nice to bump into them on the concourse at Sixfields two or three times a year and at the odd away game. Living out of teyn for so long it's also great to hear the Northampton accent being spoken areynd the greynd.

It was mere coincidence that the Cobblers' amazing unbeaten league run began the only time this season that I got all four of us to a game, but it will be a nice fact for them to recite to their own kids (if any of them ever look up from their iPads by then). The Accy match was not great but it helped to exorcise the demons of the Bradford Wembley visit that had made "Fancy coming to the Cobblers with me?" such a hard sell. Crooks in midfield looked a decent player for Stanley but we won and headed into the New Year full of confidence. Losing? That was so 2015.

January 16: Dagenham away, Won 2-1

Normal service was resumed. We played Dagenham and we won. I'll miss the trips to the Daggers, who will be two divisions below us next season. They looked quite capable of staging a recovering at the time, not least when they went 1-0 up.

But there were more great memories to add to the Victoria Road memory bank, alongside the wins with Clarke Carlisle bossing things in 2012 (goal by Tony Silva – file under short-lived geniuses, see Elad, Efon), and Ian Morris's amazing karate-style volley and Ivan Toney's overhead in 2014.

The winning volley from Ricky Holmes was a worthy way to sign off and the ensuing chorus of Spandau Ballet went down extremely well with the home stewards.

Here was a chance to see the work Chris Wilder and Alan Knill had done with the players. Rarely can a Cobbler have improved so much as Rod McDonald between the Dagenham home game and the Dagenham away game. Over a longer period we'd all seen the part where John-Joe O'Toole proved not to be the player we hoped for in his first few months. Sent out on loan to Southend, we never expected to see him again, let alone have 3,000 of us singing his name on a sunny day at Portsmouth 18 months later. JJOT is the one who looks like Jesus but it was Wilder who performed the footballing miracle of turning water into the finest claret.

February 13: Orient away, Won 4-0

This is when we knew. Until this point we *thought* we might have a good year and *hoped* we'd get it right. But after watching the second half in East London we *knew*. This was the Year of the Cobbler.

The first half was fairly cagey but the second 45 minutes was the simply unbelievable. This is what other teams do, not us.

When your centre-half (Rod McDonald) scores with an overhead kick to break the deadlock you know things are looking up. When Ricky Holmes volleys in a sublime worldy while the fans are singing 'We're gonna win the league' (check it on *YouTube*) you know it's special. When James Collins smashes in a third after 84 minutes and you've backed the Cobblers to win 3-0 you get extremely excited. When James Collins thumps home a fourth in injury-time and you still don't care and celebrate wildly anyway you know you love this team.

"I've never seen anything like it. I can't believe it," I said to another fan as we filed out with stunned grins on our faces. I don't think any of us had.

March 19: Stevenage away, Won 3-2

This was a landmark game for many fans – this was when the title looked assured. This was also when the good old Cobblers threw in a first half that took us all back to the frustrations of August.

Two poor goals were conceded to a side who had lost their previous four games. Even the sensational Adam Smith gets it wrong sometimes, but the Wilder-instilled spirit saw the yellow-clad Cobblers through after the break.

John-Joe conjured up the spirit of Ian Morris for another martial-arts finish for the equaliser and Ricky's winner, curled in off the far post after cutting in from the right, was superb. It's hard to know what was better – the goal itself, the speed with which Adam Smith was able to pile on the celebratory bundle, or the sheer joy on David Buchanan's face.

This was the game that James Collins wasn't suspended for after apologising for his indiscretions at Cheltenham. He obviously shouldn't have done it – socialising with an MK Dons player is pretty unforgiveable – but the club's decision not to punish themselves for it by letting him play paid off when he headed home our first goal.

Wilder's use of loan players throughout the season was excellent. When the main defenders had injury trouble early in the season he brought in the excellent Shaun Brisley and Darnell Furlong to shore things up after Lelan and McDonald struggled. Lee Martin added a brief attacking spark, Luke Prosser was solid insurance when the defence took more hits late in the season, while Collins and Marquis were valuable recruits when injury kept Rico sidelined for the run-in.

Holmes had (half) a season better than anything I've ever seen from a Cobblers player, continuing what seems to be something special about the club's number 11 shirt. The golden run of the sixties fascinates me even though it happened before I was born – I've got all the league programmes from that season and my favourite player, just from reading about it, was always Barry Lines, who wore 11 from the middle of the Division Four promotion season in 1960-61, all the way through to Division One in 1965-66 and back to the basement in 1969-70. Richard Hill, whose driving runs from midfield created the same sort of buzz as Holmes in Graham Carr's side, also wore 11.

April 19: Crawley home, Won 2-1

Promotion was clinched at home to Bristol Rovers, and the title came with a fourth successive draw at Exeter. I was working that day, but was there for a very rare Tuesday night home game to welcome home the champions. I'd travelled up to the game during the day to avoid the rush-hour traffic and spent the afternoon in the Sixfields Cineworld – a story in the *Sun* had suggested there would be a chance to meet the cinema-loving Cobblers squad there but the only superheroes I saw were on the foyer posters, until I reached Sixfields.

After the first deserved guard of honour of the season it was another one of those games where the Cobblers should have won 5-0 - we have about 15 of those a season in my mind – but even though the scorers were Holmes and O'Toole it was a penalty and a scramble. And of course there was another one of those brilliant free kicks that opposing teams seem to save for us. The journey back was more memorable as the M23 exit off the M25 was closed and I was still driving around the backwaters of Surrey past midnight. I don't mind doing that when we're going up (as champions) as the song says.

May 7: Portsmouth away, Won 2-1

Just surreal. A wonderful sunny day, I'd got a new phone case that charges my phone, eradicating the dead battery every away fan fears, and the atmosphere in the away end at Fratton Park was simply sensational. Supporting doesn't get better than this. The chants of 'We've Got O'Toole' have never been louder. The 23...23 undefeated became 24...24 undefeated (I was glad that one took off after sitting in front of the guys who were trying in vain to get the 22...22 version going at the Luton game – well done chaps). The inflatable-throwing at the start was worthy of the grand final of *We Are The Champions* and I've just never been so happy for such a prolonged period at a Cobblers game. The euphoria of the John Frain and Pat Gavin goals broke the meter, but both of those came after 90 minutes of stress. This is the day that will live longest with me. Amazing support, amazing team, amazing manager and a winning goal near the end right in front of us. Have that, every other season. It felt like a joyous family wedding reception at Portsmouth that day. We are a family. We are the Cobblers. And we're top of the league.

© Phil Agius

PATIENCE

by Jefferson Lake

'Maybe we could all do with being a bit more patient. With football, with our relationships, with our lives.'

Three days after Christmas 2014, two men stood in the frozen Birkenhead darkness with hate in their pockets.

In front of the main stand at Tranmere Rovers, having just watched the Cobblers lose their 12th game in a run of 15 fixtures, both my phone and that of one of the club's media men, Matt Derrig, were filled with vitriol.

Our crime? To have posted the details of this latest loss - a 2-1 defeat - on *Twitter*.

All of the responses, to my posting and to the one Matt had sent out on the club's behalf, were variations on the same theme. Some were vicious and laced with four-letter words. Some more measured. But they all ultimately said the same thing - Chris Wilder absolutely had to be sacked.

No fan was supporting him at this point. "It has gone on long enough", they said. "Surely he has to go now?" they implored.

But of course he did not. Instead he was given another transfer window, and in it signed Jason Taylor, Brendan Moloney and Ricky Holmes, all cast-offs unwanted by other clubs and all absolutely critical in turning the team around from those dark winter days.

It's standard practice when the team you cover signs a new player to speak to the reporter who covers the club from which they are arriving, to gather background information about said new signing.

In the cases of Taylor and Moloney, the reports were quite uncomplimentary; Holmes only got marginally better reviews, most of them based on his misfortune at finding himself part of a Portsmouth squad with far too many players than was sensible.

They were, of course, all vital acquisitions. Holmes provided assists and goals and Moloney was precisely the type of full-back Wilder had talked about wanting throughout his tenure - fearless, fast, good both in attack and defence.

Taylor was probably the key signing that window - an organiser and a leader who convinced those around him that they were far better than their form was currently suggesting.

It was then that I realised that one of life's clichés - and one too rarely applied in football - was very accurate indeed. Patience, in this instance and in many others over the coming months, was to prove a virtue.

The patience initially needed to be instilled in Wilder. He could easily have been sacked that winter; memories are short in football and he would have been aware that his predecessor Aidy Boothroyd was given his P45 six months after a Wembley play-off final.

The majority wanted Wilder sacked at that point, too, and retaining him (and giving him another transfer window) was a course of action which was met with lukewarm approval at best.

But the patience paid off. Just as it did with the man who became the club's player of the year in the glorious title-winning season.

On another cold northern night, this time at Rochdale after an FA Cup replay defeat, I asked Wilder both on and off the record why John-Joe O'Toole had not travelled with the squad to the game.

On the second time of asking, he threw his arms up in exasperation and was genuinely lost for words. To use his expression, he was failing to "get a tune" out of O'Toole, arguably his marquee signing the previous summer, and it was causing him immense frustration.

Because everyone knew all along that there was a fine player in there, a fact which would be proved in the second half of that season, where he hit superb form before being calamitously sent off on 'John-Joe O'Toole Day' at Mansfield.

As with Wilder, it would have been easy to cast O'Toole aside - during the bad times the only question supporters were asking was not whether the club should do so but how much it would cost, and how foolish it had been to have given him a three-year contract.

There were other illustrations of the power of patience throughout the title campaign too.

I wasn't covering the club by the time Rod McDonald was being given a chance in the side but I was reading the comments about how poor he was in his first run of matches.

By the time I got to see him in the flesh, in the vital 1-0 win at Oxford, I couldn't see how anyone could have criticised someone who basically played like a gym-enhanced Ray Warburton.

Again, it was patience that had paid dividends.

Sacking a manager every year or so hadn't been a profitable strategy for Northampton Town for decades. They'd tried it and were still a struggling fourth-tier team.

Of course, there are times when a manager has to be sacked, when it is the only course of action to prevent the catastrophe of a relegation. How different would the course of history have been if, say, Stuart Gray had been sacked with 10 games to go in 2009?

Things might have turned out differently under Chris Wilder. Moloney, Taylor and Holmes might all have been the disastrous signings they were predicted to be.

But there are too many other examples to suggest that being patient on this occasion was a fluke. Wilder, O'Toole, McDonald - they all benefited from such a policy. And ultimately so did the club and the supporters.

Maybe we could all do with being a bit more patient. With football, with our relationships, with our lives.

Because it was patience which led to the Cobblers going on a 24-match unbeaten run and winning a league championship with 99 points. And if that doesn't make it a virtue then I don't know what does.

© Jefferson Lake

BOREDOM, MISERY & JOY

by Rodney Marshall

'Memories pick out the rare nights when the home end was packed or the team beat Preston 6-0, rather than the 0-3 home defeats played out on a peat-bog pitch in front of a few hardy souls. Time does that, adding a sepia-film of charm.'

Supporting a lower division football club home and away throughout your lifetime consists of 80% boredom, 15% misery and – if you are lucky – 5% joy. Of course the percentages are not mathematically accurate and there are plenty of other emotions which come into play – hope, fear, anxiety, pride etc – but my point here is that it is those generally unexpected and sudden bursts of pure, unadulterated joy which make the long treks, the cost and the painful loyalty worthwhile. That these are shared with hundreds or thousands of other people you may have little else in common with adds a collective or communal element to the experience. This shared emotion – bordering on self-harm much of the time – makes lower league football fans a rare breed in our modern world. In the age of the 'selfie', where people spend more and more of their time locked away in a technological bubble, a virtual world of texting, tweets and surfing, the sense of genuine communal interaction is now a rarity. It is one which we should cherish.

Most professional football clubs were founded in a vanished age where Victorian or Edwardian towns and cities were often known for a specific industry: Stoke for its pottery, Luton for hat making, Sheffield for steel, or Northampton for shoes. These clubs' nicknames reflected a sense of civic pride and identity. Today these industries have either diminished or disappeared as fashions and manufacturing change, and modern cities and towns 'diversify'. However, the idea of the football club representing something important or integral within its community remains a compelling one.

I began to write this piece on a cold, sunny February morning in 2016. Northampton Town, the club I had supported since I was nine, were top of League 2 and had just announced a renewal of its 'principal club partnership' with the University of Northampton. The Vice Chancellor, Professor Nick Petford, described his pleasure at continuing to work with "a club which has been at the centre of our community for nearly 120 years." His words reflected the fact that history, tradition, continuity and the ability to offer a unique hub (in the sense of civic identity) are still seen as key elements of a local football club, even in today's global economy.

Of course towns such as Northampton are full of football fans who follow global brands such as Arsenal, Liverpool or Manchester United, clubs where joy is likely to figure at more than 5%, where you can wear the colours without being ridiculed in the school playground or office, where you are unlikely to be left worrying whether the club will survive the year or finish their incomplete stand – both genuine worries for NTFC in the 2015-16 season covered in this book. However, the glory hunter in Northampton, Luton, or Sheffield etc., forfeits the right to feel a genuine sense of communal pride when a truly special season emerges for the local league club. And doesn't that indescribable joy feel so much better when it comes, unexpectedly, after years of misery and boredom?

The early 1980s was a very different time and place. It is undoubtedly difficult for anyone under a certain age to imagine a world without internet and social media, never mind mobile phones. In terms of (lower division) football coverage, it was a desert. It was less of a problem if you lived in the town of the team you supported. The local paper – in the case of Northampton the *Chronicle & Echo* – would keep you in daily touch with transfers, speculation and gossip. However, living outside the immediate area, you might as well have been on a different planet. Miss the final scores on the Saturday BBC or ITV round-ups and I'd be left waiting for a Sunday newspaper to discover the Cobblers' result. Stuck away in the Berkshire countryside at boarding school, a midweek home match would see me queuing for the public phone at 9.20 pm to ring the club to find out the full-time score. (There was no stoppage time in those days.) The kind lady who answered calls soon got to know my voice and a frequent response to my urgent, nervous question about the result would be, "Sorry, love. The Cobblers lost one nil." With my grandmother dying suddenly, weeks after I was sent away, my parents brought my grandfather to live in London and my connection with my beloved town seemed to have been broken.

However, it was never a case of 'out of sight, out of mind'. More a question of absence, and distance, making the heart grow fonder. Unable to make it to matches during term time and now without a Northampton 'holiday home', following the club transformed itself from a hobby to an obsession. As if understanding this, the Cobblers became one of the first clubs to experiment with Sunday football, requiring a special licence to do so! This made a round trip of Bradfield to Reading to London to Northampton and back a term-time possibility, despite the seemingly timeless Sunday service limitations of British Rail.

Unwilling to restrict myself to home matches, holidays began to revolve around the complications of the British Rail timetable. Each year I'd buy the Bible-sized BR book covering every UK train line. As soon as the new fixture list winged its way from Abington Avenue Northampton to my house in South London, I would be working out whether I could make it to a midweek away match at Port Vale, Crewe, Scunthorpe, or Doncaster... (I loved the fact that FA Cup final day always appeared on the fixture list!) Train journeys represented part of the adventure. Being distanced from Northampton simply added to the glamour. Years later I lived in a ground floor flat in Exeter, a hundred metres from St James' Park. Walking to a football ground in under a minute is simply too easy, though. It cannot rival the sense I had as a teenager – or even feel today – setting out on a three hour journey to watch a match. It is football foreplay, and is often more memorable than the main event.

Simon Inglis' *The Football Grounds of England and Wales* was first published in 1983, at about the same time as my explorations of the same were becoming my major preoccupation. By now I had become possibly the only pupil to run away from boarding school because his request to attend an FA Cup second round match had been turned down. [1] I never went back and the new-found freedom of a London Sixth Form college allowed me the flexibility to travel around the country in support of the Cobblers. Financed by part-time work in a local mini-supermarket, my football away days now knew no bounds...so long as British Rail could get me back to London on the same day. This was an era in which our away turn out could often be counted on two hands, in stark contrast to the relatively large away support attracted by many lower division clubs nowadays. The world, it appears, has shrunk, or perhaps people's disposable income has increased.

Inglis' wonderful book was ground-breaking, no pun intended. Here was a man who understood the excitement of arriving by train or car in an unknown town and searching out the floodlights of the football ground; a man who appreciated football grounds for their architectural merits, including their quirky stands and ramshackle eccentricities. These have always been more evident in the 'quaint' world of lower division and non-league football.

Tragically, the Bradford fire in 1985 illustrated that 'quaint' and 'ramshackle' could sometimes equate to 'unsafe'. At Northampton Town the response to the Bradford inquest brought a knee-jerk reaction which would spell the end of the beloved County Ground, even if it somehow limped or staggered on for another decade. The likeable new chairman, Derek Banks, took the decision to collapse the main stand's roof and seated section, leaving the narrow terrace in front as the only area available. What had been a smart stand – with a newish roof and claret seats – became an eyesore, just as the club was about to wake up on the field.

As a university student, I found myself further than ever from Northampton, studying in first Cardiff and then Exeter. However, my obsession wouldn't go away. It merely changed shape. Now I used the Cobblers as a litmus test on potential girlfriends. Was she happy to come to a game? A few were. Was she willing to attend a second match after that inevitably mind-numbing debut defeat? One poor soul was and – some hundred and fifty matches later – became my wife. You are allowed to pity her, for her choice of club, or husband, or both.

Fast forward ten years from the Bradford tragedy and the Cobblers had been promoted as champions, relegated again and been through administration. Oh, and the club had moved to a smart if fairly characterless new council-owned ground on the edge of a retail park. As Inglis would reflect in his updated version of his football grounds book, Sixfields was in many ways a mirror image of the new face of football. All-seater, smaller, but with a family stand and restaurant/corporate hospitality suites, it reflected the new, sanitised version of football which slowly emerged post-Bradford fire, post-Hillsborough disaster and post Italia 90 World Cup. English football was once again attracting fans rather than fights and was becoming an increasingly trendy part of popular culture. While 'trendy' is not usually a word associated with Northampton Town FC, the move to Sixfields attracted a new breed of supporter or spectator and crowds were consistently higher than they had been at the dilapidated County Ground. Sixfields almost certainly made it easier to attract players, too.

In the final thirty years at the old ground, the Cobblers had enjoyed just two promotions. By contrast, within the first dozen years at the new stadium, Northampton had gained promotion on three occasions – subsequently relegated each time – been involved in the play-offs on five occasions and reached Wembley twice, bringing 32,000 and 40,000 'fans' to the old Twin Towers. I place fans in inverted commas because, with home crowds of between 5,000 and 6,000, many of the followers were clearly football tourists, jumping on the bandwagon for a day out in the Big Smoke. This is not intended as a criticism of these people, simply an observation. Supporters are there throughout the boredom and misery. Spectators come out when – metaphorically speaking – the sun threatens to emerge from the cloud cover. Whether we like to admit it or not, clubs require spectators as much as they need supporters and they channel most of their efforts into attracting the former. Look at the crowds enticed to unfashionable clubs such as Swindon, Fulham, Wigan, Blackpool, Bournemouth etc., in the media-hyped Premier League and a large percentage are people who weren't interested when the club was languishing in the lower leagues.

Football tourism and the increasing commercialisation of the professional game are less important aspects of the sport at lower division clubs but there is no doubt that expanded television coverage of the Football League, and the emergence of club websites and social media have transformed supporters' experience. Unlike the eighties era of me waiting nervously to ring the club to find out a result, today there are an ever-increasing number of ways to keep in touch with news at a club such as Northampton Town. Fans' forums, local newspaper websites, club sites offering match commentaries, tweets, interviews and highlights...we are constantly updated by the club itself and both informed and misinformed by fellow fans, depending on the source. For a supporter with the necessary disposable income, there has – arguably – never been a better time to be a fan of a modest-sized club: better informed away from the ground, more comfortably seated within it. We are now treated as valuable, appreciated clients...well, most of the time.

Has some of the charm of supporting a club been taken out? We have to avoid wallowing in nostalgia. It is all too easy to look back at the past with rose-tinted glasses. I tend to remember the Hotel End for its gallows-humour atmosphere and cheap entry prices, rather than its foul or racist language, leaking roof, dangerous crowd surges and disgusting open toilets. Memories pick out the rare nights when the home end was packed or the team beat Preston 6-0, rather than the 0-3 home defeats played out on a peat-bog pitch in front of a few hardy souls. Time does that, adding a sepia-film of charm. In addition, yearning for a Cobblers past is, partly, an elegy to my own lost youth. The changed back pass rule, the better playing surfaces, increased protection of skilful players, better facilities, and greater accountability demanded of clubs, in theory anyway...The supporter is 'better off', overall, even if the financial cost now makes it an expensive passion rather than an affordable pastime.

What has been lost is some of the romance. FA Cup ties used to be sacred, attracting bigger crowds and a special atmosphere, whether it was for a match against non-league opposition such as VS Rugby or European champions Aston Villa. Nowadays, even lower league clubs often put out weakened line-ups and the final itself is no longer the rousing curtain call to the domestic season. [2] The constant media and social media analysis of 'the beautiful game' has seen any mystery removed and I cannot help but feel that at times less would be more. [3] Likewise, too many modern grounds have been built in soulless settings and designed with little or no imagination. The brand new stadia constructed in some other countries put our identikit grounds to shame. Modern comfort and facilities should not come at the expense of character, creativity and individuality. Thankfully, clubs who have stayed put and rebuilt have tended to be far more imaginative, as is the case at Preston and Wolves where the grounds are now exhilarating both outside and within. Hopefully Sixfields will one day look equally impressive, albeit on a smaller scale. We can dream. It's something most lower-division football fans are good at.

****

What Northampton Town's magnificent 2015-16 season demonstrates is that a football club is not about its dilapidated terraces, sleek new stands or half-built ones. It is about everybody pulling in the same direction and, at the heart of the matter, the fans themselves.

The season had begun with a decent-looking squad assembled. Most fans were probably, like me, reasonably hopeful that the team could mount a promotion or play-off bid, without any of us being wildly optimistic. This is Northampton, after all. Although work had once again stopped on the controversial new East Stand, few fans can have expected the off-field problems of the club to escalate in the spectacular manner which they would over the next few weeks. Chairman David Cardoza's close season announcement that a London-based Indian consortium would be taking over was followed by 'radio silence' and – eventually – by news that the deal had collapsed. It seemed inevitable and many believed that the buyers had never existed. Rumours spread that the council's £10 million loan to the club had disappeared and every day seemed to bring more worrying news: police officers taking away club computers for fraud investigation, staff unpaid, players having to be paid by the PFA, a court hearing announced for unpaid tax, the council demanding full repayment of the loan. Administration and receivership were being talked about both in the local press and on social media. Remarkably, after a solid start to the season on the pitch, the increasingly bad news seemed to galvanise the players into better and better results, with the fans also turning out in force in a show of solidarity. This reached new heights in early November at the Ricoh Arena for an FA Cup tie against Coventry City, a fixture which some feared might be our final away match.

I wasn't there that day. Weeks before, unsure where my money was going and whether any cup victories or league points would be counting for anything, I took the decision not to attend any more games until the wretched mess was sorted out. Was I simply abandoning my beloved club in its hour of need? Perhaps I had simply had enough...of NTFC being misrun by yet another businessman who did not seem to care, of constant worries about whether the club had a future. There was even talk of a new phoenix club which could rise from the flames, starting off in local football. I didn't want to begin all over again, see forty years of support count for nothing, those precious moments of joy wiped off the record books. The chairman seemed to be willing to see the club go into administration and I was willing to stay away. Rightly or wrongly. I was missing a series of hard-fought wins, but the victories felt hollow, with a guillotine hanging over the club's head.

Saturday November 21st was a day which, arguably, changed both the entire season and the club's long-term future. A 2-1 away win at Notts County – a sixth success in seven league and cup matches – saw the Cobblers cement their place in the top three. Far more remarkable, though, was the manager's post-match interview. Rather than talk about the game, Chris Wilder offered an emotive plea to Cardoza to sell the club to Wilder's former employer, friend and US-based businessman, Kelvin Thomas. The interview on BBC Radio Northampton became a *YouTube* sensation and probably convinced one businessman that he needed to step aside and another that he should step in to save the club.

'I've kept quiet. And I've kept my peace about a lot of things...The players and staff are pulling rabbits out of hats and it's just remarkable how we keep going...I'm at it, I'm at it, I'm exhausted. Because there's a deal to be done. I know there's a deal to be done...that takes this club forward, that gives it a bright future, that challenges out of this division, that challenges in the next division, that challenges to try to get into the Championship. There's a deal there to be done, to get the stand built. How many more years are we going to look at that stand being empty and not earning any money?...We're playing with people's livelihoods here. There's a deal to be done, we've got to get it done. It's ridiculous. Supporters, staff, players... This football club, we can go *so* far with this football club. And I don't want to undo all the good work we've done over the past eighteen months to two years. There's a deal to be done so people can spend money and go and watch us play football. So people can come and support us and back us financially. I can't stand looking at that stand and I imagine all the supporters and the staff are the same. And I've not said anything because I've gone along with it and I've trusted that things will be looked after... We've got until next Friday. Who's going to come in? There's someone who's worked his absolute nuts off, who wants to take the club forward, who wants to put money into the club, who wants to strengthen our position as a football club, wants us to get into where we should be...wants to invest, wants to pay people's wages and wants to get the stand built and have a feel-good factor...The unity that everyone is showing in backing us is absolutely fantastic...We can't wait any longer...What's happened is an absolute shambles, a complete shambles... It's tearing us all apart...It's come to the point where I feel my voice has to be heard...Let's get the bleeding deal done.' [4]

I'd never heard or seen anything like it before. Extending to over ten minutes, it was like the defining moment in a perverse soap opera. On another level, it was a heroic speech which possibly saved our club. Within days the takeover deal was agreed, the fine form on the pitch continued and I felt that I could step back in. The passion of the manager touched the thousands of fans out there who cared and worried. Wilder's voice was heard, noted and acted upon. Amen.

My self-imposed ban now lifted, Luton away on December 12th was the day I realised that something very special was happening. In the aftermath of the Paris attacks there was a strange, brooding atmosphere in the town itself with the police out in large numbers. Kenilworth Road is like a time capsule, a blast from the past, an atmospheric but decaying football ground in a rundown area of crumbling Victorian terraces which, ironically, houses a modern, culturally-diverse population. A sold-out away end saw the packed Cobblers support standing and singing throughout as an extraordinary 4-3 victory took us top of the table for the first time all season. The atmosphere was electric and so too was the football, the festival of goals including a sublime free kick routine which would later receive more than two million *YouTube* hits and a Roy of the Rovers winner. Yes, something very special was happening. The fact that the excitement of the football, the incredible run of results and the spectacular goals being scored was all played out during and after the off-field dramas simply added spice and surrealism to the whole experience. People had suffered collectively and now the joy was communal. On the field, perhaps the most remarkable aspect was the way, having let a 3-1 lead slip, the Northampton players refused to panic, immediately stepped up a couple of gears and blitzed the home goal until the winner arrived. It was as if victory was inevitable. For the first time since Graham Carr's championship winning side of 1986-87, here was a Cobblers team which played without fear, which looked as if it could give goals away but still roar back to win. The fans, too, seemed to sense this and the raw noise generated had me mentally travelling back to the days of packed away terraces in Carr's record breaking campaign. No wonder new owner Kelvin Thomas asked the club to tweet his thanks for the away support. This was more than simply a side which *might* challenge for promotion. It felt as if we were destined to top the table.

A week later the winning run was ended by Portsmouth and we were knocked off our lofty perch. However, it was a blip, followed by ten consecutive league wins, including hard-fought victories at promotion rivals Plymouth and Oxford. Sixteen wins and two draws from nineteen league matches, by the first week in March we were top by thirteen points, twenty-one above the top play-off place and pinching ourselves. After years of boredom, despair, resignation and misery, this was unbound joy.

On Good Friday, with Premier League and Championship clubs taking an oddly-timed 'International break', the national media decided to focus on the Cobblers. The *Daily Mail* ran a feature on the club, while *The Sun* delivered a piece under the heading *Easter rising*: 'Forget Leicester – Northampton Town are English football's story of the season.' Some may disagree, but given the circumstances, in particular the climate of anxiety which had cloaked our club just a few months earlier, this had been nothing short of a miraculous season.

A couple of weeks later we had been crowned champions of League 2, a host of club records shattered, the groundsman named as the best in League 2, the goalkeeper and the manager as the best in the entire Football League, three players included in the PFA divisional side. The success stories were arriving like waves. It felt surreal and I am still pinching myself to make sure it isn't a dream.

The presentation of the trophy – with Graham Carr passing the 'torch' on to Chris Wilder – in front of a packed Sixfields, and the lap of honour which followed, represented the perfect icing on the cake. It was a derby against Luton, once again, and there was a satisfyingly cyclical feel about the occasion: twenty-three league matches unbeaten, in other words exactly half a season; a home campaign completed against the side we had beaten to go top first time around. It seemed like a clichéd plot to a Hollywood film or – as many fans observed – a fairy tale. There was a sting in the tale/tail of course, with Wilder and Knill leaving for Sheffield United a matter of days after the open-top bus celebrations. Nevertheless, they had masterminded a magical season and left the club upwardly mobile after years in the wilderness. Their departure left a sense of loss and unanswerable 'what if?' questions, but no one can take away the memories. With Rob Page appointed as the new manager a week later, a new chapter has begun.

Despite the pleasure of seeing a number of Sixfields 'sold out' signs, then the first phase of a return to a 'proper' four-sided ground, my abiding memories of the season will be the away days in the company of a veritable army of Cobblers followers packing the visitors' enclosures at Luton, Dagenham, Leyton Orient, Oxford, Stevenage, Mansfield...As the season progressed, the flavour and atmosphere of these occasions altered, from the fragile hope of those 999 at Notts County – with the benefit of hindsight, I should have made it 1,000 by being there – to the spellbound fervency at Luton and the delirious confirmation at Oxford that this *was* going to be *the* season. By then, we were travelling not simply in hope, but with excited expectation. And that – in the words of American poet Robert Frost – has made all the difference.

© Rodney Marshall

1. For the record, I was at the Priestfield stadium to see us draw with third division Gillingham and we then won a seesaw replay 3-2 to secure a third round tie with European champions Aston Villa. It felt as if the Cobblers' heroics had justified my decision to run away. Later on, various career options were turned down if they potentially got in the way of supporting the Cobblers. Even today, having hopefully mellowed with age, I hate being at work when a Northampton match is on.
2. At least this season the final was restored to the end of the season, rather than fitted in around Premier League fixtures. Nevertheless, some of the magic has gone, not helped by playing semi-finals at Wembley.
3. Despite my 'less is more' remark, the instant sharing of photos from the end-of-season Champions parade illustrates how modern technology can be magical, enabling people access to an event from the other side of the country or globe. This is discussed in the Afterword.
4. Part of Chris Wilder's 'soliloquy' – as Joe Townsend refers to it – was played at the end-of-season awards, reminding us what a pivotal, emotive moment this was in the season.

REINVIGORATED

by Tom Rostance

'We may never see a season like it again. But I - and many thousands more - have been reinvigorated by a wonderful season. And I can't wait for it all to start again.'

You see, I always knew that the second weekend of August 2015 would be pivotal in my life. I just didn't know why.

On Sunday 9th August I was married in a lovely little country house near Macclesfield. Twenty-four hours earlier John-Joe O'Toole had headed in a Dave Buchanan cross to give the Cobblers an opening-day win at Bristol Rovers. Happy days all round.

By the time I came back from honeymoon the unusual early-season optimism had already slipped. Three defeats in four games saw the Cobblers down in 16th place at the start of September.

And yet. The magical would happen. Chris Wilder's side hit the air and they would maintain flight. They would go on to amass 99 points - ninety-nine! - and win the league by 13 points. All against this backdrop of uncertainty and turmoil.

And, on top of all that, they achieved a far more impressive feat. They made me fall back in love with football again.

Allow me to explain.

****

My whole relationship with Northampton Town was predicated on a lie. My first game, on the Hotel End at the County Ground, saw us destroy Halifax 4-0, on Boxing Day 1991 in front of just over three thousand chilly folk. Naively - well, I was only eight - I assumed that this was a thing of routine. I would regularly see this group of men smash the opposition; this was going to be a piece of cake.

How wrong I was.

Over the following years my attendance at first the County Ground and then Sixfields - and then at a multitude of away ends around the lower leagues - fluctuated with a few factors. First, my elder brother's desire and inclination to take me, then a clash with a Saturday job and finally moving away for university and then work.

I would get to as many games as I could, collecting an away win maybe once every two years or so, but by 2006 I had begun a career as a football journalist which meant working nearly every Saturday. So for the last decade I have averaged between eight and ten Cobblers games a season - you can park me in the 'part-time fan' brigade if you wish.

But I would make it to the games I could. Since moving to Manchester in the summer of 2011 my attendance has been restricted to games in the north as a rule, and by the end of the 2014-15 season my passion, if we are being honest, had been dulled. Or so I thought.

The reason? Ten years of eating, sleeping, watching and discussing football for 40+ hours a week had left me rather numb to the game. Yes, I could tell you how to spell Wojciech Szczesny without looking it up, I could probably tell you how many caps Wayne Rooney had won for England or how many goals Olivier Giroud had scored, but I was beyond really caring about the game. My relationship with football was becoming functional - it was a good job, which I enjoyed - but it was a job nonetheless.

And so, while I enjoyed my last night as a free man – I was delighted that we had got off to a winning start down in Bristol – I did not have much hope or expectation about the coming season.

A few months later, just after Christmas, I was online booking a flight from Manchester to Exeter.

What had changed? Everything.

****

You can say what you like about sport being about taking part but the cold, hard facts are that nothing beats winning every week. And this was the season when we Cobblers fans finally got a chance to savour that.

And it was magnificent.

First came the hardship. As it looked like the club might actually die, despite me telling colleagues and friends at BBC Sport that 'someone always comes through to buy a football club', I spent the afternoon at Cambridge in October discussing the possible merits of starting again. Phoenix style. AFC Wimbledon style.
'We'll get to see some new grounds. Probably save a few quid...'

But, after the best bit of managerial rhetoric I can recall from a Cobblers boss after a win at Notts County a month later, the club was saved after all.
'Appeh?' You bet.

For a few amazing months I then had some insight into what it must have been like supporting Sir Alex Ferguson's Manchester United side. No matter the situation, the whole crowd - and the players and the manager - just knew we were going to win.

Take Mansfield away for example. A glorious sunny day at Field Mill in March. Chris Wilder plays three target men up front in a 4-3-3 formation for the first time all season and we are 2-0 down before I've had time to make a dent in my pre-match Chicken & Balti.

In any other season of following the Town the away end would have been a mixture of gallows humour, outright disdain and a shrugging acceptance of defeat.

Instead, at half-time the only question doing the rounds at the urinal was how many we would eventually win by. On came Ricky Holmes, soon it was 2-2 and, while we ended up taking just a point back down the M1, this team's mentality had once again proven itself.

It was the same on that superb afternoon at Kenilworth Road. Always a highlight for me as a fan, thanks to the frankly ludicrous entrance to the away end and a great combination of proximity to home and usually potent atmosphere.

This time it was different. The game fell on the weekend of my birthday and we made a day of it, sharing an executive box with a friend of mine who is a Luton fan. I would literally get cold feet - I wasn't permitted to wear trainers so had to leave them at the front desk and walk in in just my socks - and the team looked like following suit soon after half-time when they let a 3-1 lead slip and the Hatters drew level.

Again, the setback was no problem. On came Ricky Holmes for his first appearance since August, three touches later he whistled in a 25-yarder and the Cobblers won 4-3. We were top of the league for the first time since 1991. The first time in my 25 years of following.

Neither me, nor my long-suffering brother, really believed that we would stay there. I ran into the *Chronicle & Echo*'s Jeremy Casey later that night in the County Tavern, slightly worse for wear. He told me that the Cobblers would sign a striker in January and win the league by 10 points. I told him he was mad.

And so it went on.

I saw victories at Morecambe and at Oxford; at York and Carlisle. We won 10 games in a row. My new wife had to be told that any spare weekends I could get off work were now to be dedicated solely to this title charge. The promise that this was a one-off will hopefully be broken.

As the season rolled on and the wins racked up, friends from university, from old jobs, from school who I'd not spoken to in years, started getting in touch. One of the beauties of following a small team is that you are always associated with that club in the minds of your footballing friends.

I'm the only Northampton fan most of them will ever meet. So I became - as we all did - part of the story.

People at work would congratulate me after each win, as if I'd played a blinder in centre-mid. I'd receive text messages asking what on earth was going on, emails asking just what Chris Wilder was up to.

The surreal year rolled on until I made that flight to Exeter for the aforementioned final game of my season. Flying to a League Two match. It sounds as bizarre now as it felt at the time. But the memories of that afternoon, of this season, will live with me forever. I'm sure of that.

Since I've been married, Northampton Town have lost five league games. Two of those came before I'd even landed from my honeymoon. We won 28 league games, including 10 in a row, and ended the season 24 unbeaten.
Chris Wilder may have left. We may never see a season like it again. But I - and many thousands more - have been reinvigorated by a wonderful season.

And I can't wait for it all to start again.

© Tom Rostance

CHAMPIONIES!
Olé, Olé, Olé!

by Norman Maycock

'I never expected to experience a season like this again. Sure, we hope every August, but it's more out of habit. The default position to assume. We don't really expect even a fraction of what's happened.'

Very occasionally, something remarkable happens if you're a Cobblers fan. Some of us have been lucky enough to have experienced three Championships and three Wembley appearances, but some, born at the wrong time, may have had to wait thirty years for something extraordinary to occur, pecking at crumbs on the way. Others make the wrong choices, move away, lose interest, join the choir invisible, and tramp another uncertain path under an arid sky.

Imagine this scenario for example. (Certain facts have been changed to protect the innocent.) It is summer 1976. Hottest since the last hottest. The Racecourse is like the Gobi desert. A dustbowl. A travelling salesman from Penge, specialising in seersucker shirts, racks up in town. On a good day, he can shift six dozen. Tired of life on the road, he longs for somewhere to hang his hat, tether his afghan. Arbitrarily, he decides this town is El Dorado. Admittedly he is drunk when he makes this decision. He is introduced to the Cobblers after being struck on the head by a wayward clearance from Stuart Robertson over the main stand as he walks down Abington Avenue, carrying a bag of dried fish. Dazed and lacking judgement, but thinking it an omen, he impulsively decides to buy a regular season ticket. Ten years later and desolate, he inherits a chicken farm of 600 acres in Des Moines, Iowa, from his first cousin twice removed. He feeds his season ticket to his rabid hound, and leaves on the midnight train. Ironically, Graham Carr is just assembling his all-conquering team at this very moment. His patience ran out. He thought that life was a journey, not a destination. He'd read it in a book. In three years' time, he boasted three million chickens running wild, but many said he was counting the same chicken three million times, others that he was counting his chickens before they hatched. Trevor Morley and Richard Hill were running wild, that's all that mattered to me. Wrong time, wrong place, wrong choice. The crazy fool thought it was about enjoyment, not endurance. It's a cautionary tale to all the faint-hearted out there in the wild blue yonder. Just hang on in there.

Unwavering, engrossed, addicted since 1962 when as a 13 year old I started going up to the County Ground, now almost beyond memory, the adventure began. My only contact with live sport previously had been seeing Pat Smythe fall off Flanagan at Timken's Show. From a toddler I'd hitherto followed the Cobblers listening to *Sports Report*, Saturday at 5 o'clock, and then waiting for *The Green 'Un* to be delivered. Flag-Kick's reports were devoured, read and re-read. In those days there were no score updates, no half-times, no inflection in the voice of the announcer reading out the results. A state of unbearable tension gripped us all. Dad would check his pools coupon. He got eight draws once, but there were forty-three that week and his winnings amounted to minus four and six. Mum would open a tin of pilchards for tea, until someone hid the tin opener; Grandad would come round to watch *Dixon of Dock Green*, then spend hours staring into the fire, uttering not one word until it was time for him to go home. He was trying to remember what he was trying to forget. He was an old salty dog, who showed off his barnacles with pride. He was of that generation where words are superfluous.

Unbeknownst to me at the time, I'd stumbled on a wonderful season. 'Remarkable' was about to unfold. School seemed unreal. I felt like an extra in a bad 'B' movie. Algebra, Physics, Latin, bored me rigid. It was *Pythagoras This* and *Aristotle That* and *Horace How's Your Father*, but one Tuesday in balmy September it was Cobblers 8 Wrexham 0, and the following Monday, it was 7-1 versus Halifax Town. And still the crowd called out for more. It started snowing on Boxing Day, and didn't stop till March. A proper winter. If your pipes hadn't frozen, you just weren't trying. The whole town reeked of paraffin. John Kurila was suspended for three weeks and never missed a game; it could have been six weeks, he still wouldn't have missed one. Which was only fair because it was an icy pitch at Meadow Lane that day when he got sent off. Big John just lost his footing and sailed horizontally through the air like an Exocet missile and of course his studs were raised, but the Notts County player's shin, or was it chin, just happened to be there, that's all. What I do remember is when the club tried out a new song, a funereal dirge, an aid to constipation, sung to the tune of 'Daisy Daisy'. It was like The National Anthem. Rank. Halfway through, you lost interest. You lost the will to live. By the time the Hotel End finished singing the turgid lament, the Cobblers were usually three up.

When the thaw came, the team emerged out of moth-balls, but continued relentlessly their path to the Division 3 Championship. 109 goals. It was absurd. The genius of Dave Bowen then came to the fore. He knew this was unsustainable. Too many turnips in the onion bag. The bubble had to burst. The bar had been set too high, the goalposts too wide. The corner flags even faced the wrong way. The expectations of the fans needed to be tempered. He allowed net-busters Cliff Holton, Alec Ashworth and Frank Large to leave. He needed a better balance between defence and attack, so brought in Charlie Livesey, Ken Leek and Joe Broadfoot. He needed forwards who couldn't hit a cow-shed door with a double bass. The defence were getting complacent. They knew the forwards would bail them out. Chic Brodie had even started to learn The Knowledge out on the pitch, memorising whole tracts of routes throughout London, anticipating the time when he hung up his doggone boots to become a cabbie. Dave was a contrarian. He was a bear. He guided the club into Division 1 without flamboyance, concentrating on teamwork, quietly assembling a side below the radar. Joe Kiernan was a class act but virtually unknown outside the town. Likewise Don Martin.

Is it just a coincidence that Alf Ramsey also discarded his prime goalscorer, Jimmy Greaves, during The World Cup? And is it just fanciful that Jack Charlton's Irish side was a copy of Graham Carr's 1986-87 team? In retrospect, it's hard to comprehend how a small unfashionable club had so much influence on the world scene. That Gary Mabee's End-of-Season videos were sought after and pored over from the San Siro to the Maracana. That the iconic sight of Carl Heggs whirling his shirt round his neck like a demented banshee one December night in Basingstoke would be replicated on so many football fields thereafter. I was frozen to the marrow that night, but it was my own fault for taking a marrow with me. The steward searching me thought I was just pleased to see him. And that memorable passage in Lionel Messi's autobiography when as an 11 year old and affected by serious health issues, the child prodigy locked himself in his bedroom and watched, mesmerised, on a continuous loop, Sean

Parrish's solo goal v Cardiff City, and John Frain's free-kick at Wembley, fuelling his ambition to continue his dream. 'Eck en llamas, lo dulce de un pie izquierdo.' (Blooming ada, what a sweet left foot.) 'Voy a ir a los pies de nuestros escaleras y masticar un trozo de cartilago de bufalo.' (I'll go to the foot of our stairs and chew on a shard of buffalo gristle.) To think that we played a small part in his career is truly humbling.

By 1967, the Cobblers were back in Division 3. But the legacy was a line drawn in the sand for our generation. It was like when Robert Redford exclaimed to Meryl Sheep in *Out of Africa*, 'You've spoilt it for me, being alone.' The past few years had spoilt it for all of us. After witnessing the cream, Bobby Charlton, Dave Mackay, George Best, Bobby Moore, and dozens more, how could you view what followed, except in a different way? And all to the soundtrack of Rubber Soul, Revolver, Blonde on Blonde, Jimi Hendrix, The Stones. The music of the years gone by. Of course, it wasn't all good. The miracle of the 60s wasn't The Cobblers getting to Division One, rather *Puppet on A String* getting to Number One. I was 17. I left town for good. No regrets. No tears goodbye. But I left the best part of me there, the holy innocent part. And also a fantastic collection of Dinky Supertoys in their original boxes.

But where are the snows of Yesteryear?

****

So it's 30 years since Graham Carr's all conquering side, and 54 since I started treading the duckboards, and I never expected to experience a season like this again. Sure, we hope every August, but it's more out of habit. The default position to assume. We don't really expect even a fraction of what's happened. Since I left town, every game is an away game now. Sometimes, on those long trips up north, it seems more an exploration of man's loneliness in the face of an indifferent universe, than attending a game of football, all those nocturnal ramblings in strange, god-forsaken towns. Ten thousand miles spent roaming around, following some wonderful dream. There's something indescribably magnificent about it. It happens occasionally when you're on yet another train station at midnight, an owl is hooting; you gaze up at the heavens and the moon is shining bright as Charlie Parker, there's Ursa Major twinkling back at you and you're very close to discovering the eternal truths about man's existence. It's magical, something to do with the human spirit conquering all, and then a man walks by with a tray of pies, and you think that deep thoughts can wait for another day. Man's eternal conflict between pie and profundity.

Even in long life, one never knows what is coming next, joy or tribulation. Happiness, so often sought in vain, arrives unsought in the most unexpected ways, and so swiftly flies away. They are not long, the days of wine and roses. I'd just finished a watercolour the morning of the Leyton Orient away game. 'Moose in repose under a vanilla sky', (After Landseer), and was feeling pretty good. The moose was a metaphor for the decline of western civilisation. The hustle and bustle of Leyton High Street with its rich variety of sights and sounds conspired to add to an optimistic vibe in the air. Leyton in February. Another one ticked off the bucket list. I sat amongst the home fans as I like to do, as I have always done for over 40 years, ever since it became apparent away supporters were invariably shoved behind the goal, the worst place from where to view a game. You have to be discreet of course. Deadpan, barely alive, a mere shadow. Merge into the background. It's best to wear beige. So when Rod's overhead kick went in, the chap next to me groaned, and I groaned too, though my heart was aflame with pride. When Ricky's goal of the century went in, the chap next to me shouted, 'Fluke!' so I yelled 'Lucky pot!' But when the match ended 4-0, he nudged me in the solar plexus and whispered, 'Fair play to Northampton, they right done us over', so I replied, 'And to think they almost went bust in the autumn'. So we strolled back to the tube and we agreed they were the best side in the league, apart from Oxford of course, and he asked if I would be coming to the next game, and I said 'yes', and then he said 'Well to be honest I'm really a Cobblers fan pretending to be an Orient fan' and I said I was too, and then he said the whole row in front of us were Cobblers fans in disguise. He recognised some as old muckers from Burton Latimer who used to race whippets in the late 70s, one guy drove a meat truck in Daventry, there were two grass widows, the Thistle sisters, who ran a gambling den in Shutlanger, there was Pete, a part-time podiatrist from Pattishall, some he knew from his street, some were old school chums, one was his milkman, one was his own mother. Many carried false I.D. in case they were frisked by overzealous stewards. One was dressed as The Phantom of the Opera but no-one ever found out why.

That week seemed crucial. I thought we would lose all three games against Orient, Oxford, and Wycombe, yet we won all three. Thereafter, the second TV set was permanently on Ceefax red button, League 2 table. Twenty four 7. I constantly stared at it in wonderment, disbelief. Whenever the latest soap opera, drama, documentary, or news programme palled, and appalled, I just shifted the gaze to the other TV, and the cherry blossom was in bloom again. The mountain moon with her pure light entered the room.

One problem I can foresee after such a stunning season, especially for the younger supporter, for whom success is another country, is the difficulty coping with the future when we re-assemble in August and the team may initially falter in the higher echelons. Called the 'Neil Armstrong Syndrome', named after the astronaut and his fellow moon-walkers, who found it impossible to adjust to the banality of everyday life on their return to Earth, it describes being unable to cope with the demands of wives, the bleating of children, the gossip of neighbours, the cynicism of politicians, the complacency of goldfish. This season we've been to the moon, the stars, and the stratosphere. This is unchartered territory for a lot of fans. Ahead lies uncertainty. A new manager adds an extra dimension.

I have e-mailed Kelvin Thomas asking if he would be willing to fund and set up counselling sessions and workshops throughout the summer. Attendance would be voluntary of course, refreshments provided, albeit of a basic nature in order to discourage freeloaders. Clarence would welcome each fan with a lovely big monster hug. Reassuring club officials would mingle, patting shoulders and offering solace if required. A hologram of the match day announcer, bellowing incoherently, would kick-off the evening to relax everyone. A minute's applause would follow, gratuitous, but now part of the match day experience. Role play would be a key ingredient. Fans attending would disperse into different groups and work diligently through various scenarios. Experts schooled in meditation, mindfulness, stress management, would be able to offer techniques to allay the disappointment of losing the manager, losing key players, losing games, now almost a distant memory. 'Grasp the opportunity of the new dawn. Relish the past but don't dwell on it. A dead goat fears not the butcher's knife'. These themes and their implications would be discussed frankly but hopefully without rancour. A dossier of discarded Alan Knill free kick routines, found in an old shoe box, would be available for perusal, including one where the ball is passed back 70 yards to Adam Smith, who, like an archer of old (not Jordan) would arrow the ball like a rocket into the opponents' net. Only to be tried with strong favourable prevailing winds. The evening would end with group hugs, and a rendition of 'Fields of Green'. A certificate would be presented to each fan, plus a small bag of desiccated coconut to keep blood sugar levels up on the way home. The match day announcer would still be bellowing incoherently as the fans disperse. And to think all these years we thought it was the PA system that was at fault.

For the Luton game, I was relegated to the East Stand. I rang up a hundred times one day for a ticket, but the glory hunters had got there first. Not that I'm bitter. Strangely, I enjoyed the change of scenery enormously. Being nearer to the pitch added to the atmosphere. The sight of a packed West Stand pretty impressive. Hadn't been in the East since the infamous sink hole appeared against Fulham. Jim Stannard dived for a save and had to be dug out. (They say after the game he added a codicil to his will insisting on being cremated). I had to ask directions. I was out of my comfort zone. My bag was searched, a cheese sandwich viewed with suspicion, though I got the impression the steward was auditioning for a role. Normally I'm just waved through. The grey hair and long suffering demeanour always sways it. Groups of men drinking from paper cups stood sheltering from the storm, huddled, like characters in a Lowry painting. Muttering inanities. It seemed very third world. The skies darkened, the heavens opened, the rain poured like a distant shadow, representing the recent troubling times. Then bright sunshine as the players came out. It was a masterful touch by the club, incredibly moving and symbolic, much appreciated by us poor relations in the East. But at least I didn't have to get up five minutes before half-time to allow a few burly souls, visibly salivating, first pickings of the pies, obscuring the view of the first goal, and repeat the practice five minutes before the end to enable them to get a quick getaway from the car park, thus obscuring the view of another goal. It all seemed rather civilised this side of the pitch, us bathed in sunshine, the chap next to me asking if we were the team in red. Chris Wilder even turned and gave us a wave at the end during the presentations. How grateful we were as we strained to see what was going on. Not that I'm bitter.

The Cobblers were magnificent, a joy to behold, as they had been all season. But I felt sad that it was all over. Blue and downhearted. That the like of this I would never see again. A magical season which could never be repeated. The sorrow of parting, a strange taste that lingered in the heart, as I clambered up the grassy bank after the celebrations. 'The willow twig will never again be green', a man said as I boarded the train. The greater the love, the more tragic when it's over.

And how I've loved it all. The best of times of course, but also the worst of times. The achievements in the Sixties stand alone to those who were around then. It's crazy to make comparisons with that era. This season though seems so much more intense than 30 years ago. Then, the team was also wonderful. Trevor Morley and Richard Hill will always be spoken of in hallowed terms, as will Graham Carr, but now we have so much more encompassing the games. The live commentaries, the interviews, the internet websites, the *Twitter* feeds, the trolling, the highlights on TV and online at the click of a mouse. How times change. Once it was the print edition of the *Chronicle & Echo* you turned to in order to find out the latest news. Now it's the last place you visit, if you bother at all. It's already out of date. It must be strange if a fan is not online. These poor souls must have to engage with a real human being to get any information, always slightly disconcerting.

So it's goodbye to one of the greatest seasons of all time, and on to fresh adventures. Let's celebrate this team for evermore. What a time we've had. The vocabulary hasn't been invented to do it justice. But it will remain within us always. We knew in our hearts Chris was just passing through. Here today, gone tomorrow, like John Nott. But as he presided over such a special time in our history, his star will never fall. Perhaps he will be proposed for 'Legend' status at the next Trust meeting and a bronze statue commissioned, or at least a papier mâché bust, if funds won't stretch that far. It was worth the long, long wait for this moment to arise, and of course we forgive you for leaving. Sheffield United will now be my second favourite club. Until you leave there of course.

But my first club will be my first club forever...

© Norman Maycock

THE KING IS DEAD, LONG LIVE THE KING

by Jeremy Casey

'There were stories of the good, the bad and the ugly of football, but there was never a dull moment from the day the players reported back for pre-season. It was non-stop'

The King is dead, long live the King.

After a final mad, mad week of what was a mad, mad season at Sixfields, that was perhaps a phrase the Cobblers supporters were having to get their head around.

Because just a matter of hours after revelling in the joyous open-top bus champions parade that peaked with the team being hailed by thousands of jubilant supporters in the Market Square, those same fans were stunned by the news that their team's manager was quitting.

Yep, Chris Wilder, the cheerleader supreme on that open top bus, a man who looked like he was enjoying the day more than anybody else in Northampton, was leaving the Cobblers and heading back to his roots to take over as boss of Sheffield United. And he was taking assistant Alan Knill with him.

A week later, Port Vale boss Rob Page was quitting his own job and stepping into Wilder's sizeable shoes at Sixfields. It was a remarkable and unexpected twist in the tale of an amazing 10 months at Northampton Town Football Club.

As a fan, it was a roller-coaster ride. A season of ups and downs, worry and awe, fantastic football, brilliant goals and superb supporters. As a journalist, it was the season that just kept on giving, with story after story after story coming out of the club. So much so, that at times it was hard to keep up!

There were stories of the good, the bad and the ugly of football, but there was never a dull moment from the day the players reported back for pre-season. It was non-stop, from the Ivan Toney transfer saga in July, to the East Stand redevelopment saga, the autumn financial crisis, the takeover, the players performing superbly on the pitch to win promotion, the league title and then, finally, Wilder leaving and being replaced.

That was the final surprise of a season packed full of them. Anybody who saw Wilder enjoying himself during that champions' parade will still be struggling to get their head around the fact that just hours later he was discussing his departure, but he was, and he ended up at Bramall Lane.

And who can really blame him for that? The Blades may be playing in the same division as the Cobblers in 2016/17, but that is pretty much where the similarities between the clubs end - as United are a very big fish in a pretty average-sized pond, with average gates touching 20,000. That alone would have meant Cobblers supporters would have understood the move and most do, but then there was Wilder's 'steel city' connections:
He was born in Sheffield.
He lives in Sheffield.
He is a former Sheffield United player.
He is a lifelong Sheffield United supporter.

As a set of reasons for taking the job go, they were pretty convincing ones.
But the move was still a blow for the Cobblers fans. After all, Wilder was the man who had just masterminded one of the most momentous seasons in the long history of Northampton Town. And it wasn't just about his efforts with the players and the magic they produced on the pitch virtually every time they played. It was also about what he did off the pitch, playing a huge and decisive role in the club continuing to exist after the nightmare of the financial woes in October and November.

This kind of scenario is nothing new for lower league clubs, who regularly see their managers working wonders, enjoying success, and then being picked off by bigger clubs with deeper pockets. Just look at Burton Albion, who have lost both Gary Rowett (to Birmingham City) and Jimmy-Floyd Hasselbaink (to Queens Park Rangers) in the space of two years - yet they have still managed to win back-to-back promotions, so it need not be a negative for the club left behind.

Losing a successful boss is not a new thing for the Cobblers either, as the most recent time the club won promotion before this year, back in 2006, Colin Calderwood upped sticks and joined Nottingham Forest within a matter of weeks. It's just the way football works.

There will be Cobblers fans who may still be struggling to understand why Wilder left a club on the up, with a cracking playing staff, all under contract, and has a stable infrastructure behind the scenes. But it is Wilder's call, and the pull of his home town proved too strong to resist. There is the size of the club as well. Sheffield United is a genuine sleeping giant, with 12,000 season tickets already sold for next season. They are in a slump at the moment, and are now preparing for their sixth straight season in the third tier of English football, but Wilder clearly believes he can succeed where other managers have failed.

There will be some Cobblers fans who may be bitter that Wilder has walked out on the club, angry that he has jumped ship - but they shouldn't be bitter, or angry. Disappointed? Yes. Upset? Yep. Frustrated? Yep. But angry? No. That's because Wilder doesn't owe Northampton Town anything; indeed, if anything it is the Cobblers that owe him.

It is only 28 months ago that Wilder left Oxford United to take over a Cobblers team on the brink of the non-League abyss, six points adrift at the bottom of Sky Bet League Two and looking doomed. He was entrusted by then chairman David Cardoza to pull off the great escape, and he did it. It is pure speculation to imagine where Northampton Town FC would be now if they had been relegated in 2014, but I think it's safe to assume the consequences wouldn't have been pretty.

A fairly mediocre season followed if truth be told, and Wilder may well have been in danger of losing his job in what was a pretty bleak mid-winter of 2014, with the Cobblers suffering a run of eight defeats in nine games in all competitions. There were no hints of the magical season that was to follow at that point, but Wilder didn't pack up, Cardoza kept his nerve and his faith in the manager. Wilder set about putting things right.

And how. In the second half of the campaign there were glimpses of what was to come, with the acquisition of the likes of Ricky Holmes, Brendan Moloney and Jason Taylor proving key - as well as a change in playing style - which brings us to the 2015/16 season.

On the pitch it has been a bit of a dream, the team playing great football, scoring great goals, and breaking club record after club record on their way to winning the title by 13 points. Wilder was the architect of the team, but that is only the half of it when it comes to his contribution to the very survival of the club.

We all know how close the club came to going out of existence back in the dark days of November. The fact that the club is still here, and that those thousands of supporters were able to line the streets to acclaim their champions after the season had been completed - a lot of that is down to Wilder. During all the chaos and confusion, he kept the players focused, he kept spirits and morale high around the club, fielded question after question after question about takeovers and the money troubles. He even worked for three months without pay, as did his assistant Knill and the rest of the coaching staff, and it would have been easy for him to wash his hands of everything and walk away. But he didn't.

Wilder also played a major role in enticing Kelvin Thomas into buying the club, and he made that unforgettable speech following an excellent 2-1 win at Notts County in November. A speech that, it is no exaggeration to say, probably led to the club being saved, with Cardoza eventually coming to his senses and selling up. There is so much that Cobblers supporters should be thanking Wilder for.

As a Cobblers fan of more than 40 years, I am as disappointed as anybody that Wilder has left the club as I think he really could have achieved great things if he stayed. But I don't blame him for going. We all know how fickle football can be, and as a manager there are only certain moments in your career when you are 'hot property', and for Wilder that moment is now. He did so well with the Cobblers that Sheffield United came calling, and it was a call he couldn't refuse.

Wilder is ambitious, wants to manage at as high a level as he can, and he feels there is more potential with the Blades than there is at Northampton, and that can't be argued with. So I wish him well.

For me, there is no doubt Wilder can leave Sixfields with his head held high, and with his part in the history of this club writ large. Wilder will, of course, return to Sixfields next season, but will be heading for the visitors' dugout when he rocks up with the Blades. And when he does, I can't imagine his reception being anything other than a rousing one from the grateful Cobblers supporters. Which is exactly what he deserves. He has been the man behind a season that will never be forgotten, no matter what happens from here on in.

Certainly in all my years of watching the Cobblers, the 2015/16 season was up there with the very best I have seen, vying for top spot with the title-winning campaign of 1986/87. If I had to choose one, I would probably pick Wilder's team over Carr's as the best I have seen - but then if you ask me next week, I might change my mind! They are that closely matched.

So what of the future? One of Wilder's mantras (and there were quite a few of them!) throughout the season, and particularly the troubled times, was that the 'club and the supporters will be here long after I have gone, and long after the players have gone'. Well, thankfully, that is very true.

Wilder's departure is definitely Northampton's loss and could, of course, end up being Sheffield United's gain, but this need not be a downer for the Cobblers, with Chairman Thomas quick to appoint Rob Page as the new man to take the reins. Now I don't have a crystal ball. I can't predict the future, and I can't sit here and declare that Page is going to be a successful manager at Sixfields. He could be. He could turn out to be the best manager the club has ever had. I certainly hope he is just that of course, and he is a young, ambitious manager who has a decent track record in his short career to date. He has only ever managed in League One, and in his 20 months at the helm at Port Vale he lifted the club from the relegation zone when he took control, to a 12th-place finish in his first full season in charge. Page did that on a limited budget, and although Thomas won't talk about figures, it seems pretty certain the former Wales international defender will have a few more pennies to work with at Sixfields. It's not going to be a pot of gold as the club isn't going to be spending beyond its means, but he will have money to spend to strengthen, and he is walking into a club that boasts a confident, exciting, energetic and talented squad of players.

There is momentum, and it will hopefully be maintained. It has been an exciting time to be a Cobblers fan, that cannot be argued, but who's to say it won't get even more exciting from here on in? Matching or bettering what has happened over the past year or so will take some doing, but it's not beyond the realms of possibility.

I doubt there was a single Cobblers supporter in June 2015 that will have been sitting there thinking, 'We are going to win League Two by 13 points next season... and end the campaign on a 24-match unbeaten run playing some amazing football.' I doubt there are many sitting there in June 2016 thinking the team will storm League One either. But you never know do you? We can always dream. Thanks to Wilder and his magnificent players, plenty of dreams came true for the Cobblers' loyal supporters over the past 12 months. Now it's over to Page and the boys in claret and white to try and make those dreams come true all over again, and you can guarantee the Town supporters will get behind their new man just like they got behind Wilder.

The King is dead, long live the King. Up the Cobblers.

© Jeremy Casey

OBLIVION TO LEAGUE ONE: NORTHAMPTON TOWN'S INCREDIBLE SEASON

by Joe Townsend

'Supporters value passion and commitment almost as high as results. That makes this season extra special for Cobblers fans.'

BBC Radio Northampton reporter Joe Townsend penned this article after the Cobblers' 2-2 draw with Bristol Rovers sealed promotion with five games still to play. A shorter version appeared on the BBC football website as 'Northampton Town: From the Brink of Oblivion to League Two Promotion' on 09/04/2016.

Northampton has had its football club since 1897. In November it very nearly lost it. Five months on, the Cobblers are the first Football League team to be promoted in 2016, and on the verge of ending a 29-year title drought.

From exhausting to enthralling. That just about sums up this season.

Back in November, outstanding repayments on a £10.25m loan were being called in by the Borough Council as they petitioned for Northampton Town to be put into administration. Now that's a lot of money. Enough to pay the annual fuel bill for 7,900 people - a sold-out Sixfields Stadium. Ironic.

Ten million. It wasn't a figure you could escape from around Northamptonshire, indelibly etched on the psyche of every casual observer as much as that 20-minute Wembley capitulation against Bradford in 2013 is on Teyn fans. Adebayo Akinfenwa couldn't save the Cobblers then, and try as he might, he couldn't now. [The first successful bid for his shirt on the online auction was £7500 but the bidder couldn't pay up. Second time around it raised £440.]

That number really was *everywhere*. Eight figures that transcended sport in the county, giving its professional football club unwanted national attention.

But, in actual fact, the much smaller £166,000 tax bill and consequent winding-up hearing was the real danger. With Northampton Town's bank account frozen, there existed an imminent threat of oblivion.

This wasn't exactly what I had in mind if I'm honest. Plenty of supporters made sure they told me straight that I too would be out of a job if the

Cobblers went bust. Brackley, Corby, Kettering, AFC Rushden & Diamonds and Daventry would've been the alternative in reality. But with respect, the job description at BBC Radio Northampton in January 2015 said 'patch contains only English town with professional cricket, rugby *and* football'.

I've never liked being dragged round the shops on a Saturday afternoon. Luckily for every Northamptonian, I don't think Chris Wilder has either, a veteran of 700 managerial games; not forgetting the long playing career prior. Cue an impassioned pitch-side rant at Notts County. Trust me, it was more soliloquy than interview. I tentatively held out that microphone, just far enough away to feel safe... Well, safeish.

"I get pulled up about that a lot," grinned Wilder nostalgically. "It'll stick with me for a long time, possibly as long as I'm in football management. There's a time for honesty in football. That was one of them."

It's certainly something I'll never forget. A manager publicly speaking out against his employer takes real courage but more, that person has to really care about their football club. Supporters value passion and commitment almost as high as results. That makes this season extra special for Cobblers fans.

"We'd kept quiet for a long time; possibly far too long," Wilder explained. "People weren't getting paid, so I spoke for the players and staff, hopefully the supporters as well. There was a great reaction. Obviously, things moved on very quickly after that and if I played a little part in it then great."

Something of an understatement. Forty-eight hours later and former Oxford United chairman Kelvin Thomas had agreed a takeover from David Cardoza. Wilder's players then stepped into another gear; they've lost just one league game since.

That defeat, inflicted by promotion rivals Portsmouth, was a bad idea in hindsight. The Cobblers then won 10 in a row, equalled a fourth tier record of eight successive away victories, and remain unbeaten in 19 games.

Such form has ended a decade-long wait for promotion. Back then BBC Radio Northampton summariser Lee Harper was in the Cobblers goal.

"I remember the adulation after beating Chester City to go up, that's the overriding memory of what was a fantastic season," said Harper. "This season, when I did my first game away at Barnet in August, I never saw this coming."

Let's be honest Harps, neither did Cobblers fans, did they? Well, at least not with you in the commentary booth. Do you remember those first five games you did?

"I was actually getting a bit of stick on *Twitter* for being a bad luck omen, and I'm a superstitious guy so I do think about those sort of things."

For the record, I don't. Thankfully before Lee asked for his P45 he got his win at Wycombe on 3 October and hasn't seen the Cobblers lose in League Two since.

"I thought they'd go close because there was quality in the team, but with all the turmoil going on off the pitch, it didn't look like it would go their way," Harper continued. "But the fans' reaction to it all is what's galvanised the club and not just the club, but the whole town of Northampton. I have to be honest, I don't think anyone envisaged this."

The Cobblers are the highest goalscorers in League Two with 73, and have scored three or more goals a staggering 14 times in all competitions this season, drawing a blank in just five of 48 matches.

"The side I played in and Chris Wilder's are very different," added Harper. "Under Colin Calderwood we were very defensively strong and set up to be difficult to beat. I mean we had some good players, but this team at the moment, it's really offensive football. They just score goals for fun, and play with a real style - it's been a pleasure to watch them this year. Our achievement was great, but people only remember champions, and this current Cobblers team deserve that. They deserve to be remembered for what they've achieved this season, especially given the circumstances they've achieved it in."

Long before Doomsday at Meadow Lane on 21 November, Sixfields wasn't the happiest of places. A home defeat by Dagenham left Northampton Town 16th on the first Saturday in September; already eight points off the pace. Supporters demonstrated against the ownership the following weekend, and the lack of progress on the unused, concrete East Stand at the ground, a development 18 months behind schedule.

Two thousand claret and white seats are open for business there now, while three more wins would see Wilder's side pass the haul of Graham Carr's 1987 Cobblers team to join York, Swindon and Plymouth as fourth-tier centurions.

"It's been an unbelievable effort," said a proud Wilder. "Everybody in and around the club during that difficult period deserves enormous credit. To think the players kept up great performances, and staff got on with their jobs while not getting paid is phenomenal. Managers come and go, players come and go, but supporters and the football club will remain. I always said survival of the football club was the first and foremost thing. It'll just be great if we can put the icing on the cake and add a title that we really deserve. No big interview this time though - I'll have my head in the fridge."

I think he's earned that beer. A BBC Radio Northampton interview is in the contract though, Chris. I'll be sure to keep a sage distance.

© Joe Townsend

HEROES

by Martyn Ingram

'I managed to buy a turnstile from the Hotel End on *eBay*. I had it restored and repainted and it has pride of place in my back garden. It is at times such as these that it is handy to have an understanding wife.'

On Easter Monday 1964, my elder brothers and their girlfriends thought it would be fun to take me to Portsmouth for the day from Northampton, look over HMS Victory and then perhaps go to Fratton Park where the Cobblers were playing. I hadn't been to a game before. That day was pivotal in my life. Had HMS Victory not been closed for the Bank Holiday, then maybe I would have run away to sea, but as the Cobblers were the only entertainment on offer I was saved from a life of swabbing the deck – I went to the game and absolutely loved it.

The team I saw that day was the nub of the team that would gain promotion in the following season and then compete at the top level of the English game against the likes of Wolves, Burnley and Tottenham – all teams that had won the title within the previous few seasons – along of course with Manchester United, Arsenal, Liverpool and Leeds.

Brian Harvey was in goal at Portsmouth, Theo Foley, Mike Everitt and Terry Branston at the back, Derek Leck and John Kurila at half back (midfield to you), Tommy Robson on the wing, Jim Hall up front with Billy Best and Bobby Hunt…all of those players played in the top flight.

They were my first heroes.

In 1968 my family moved to Southampton but I kept my allegiance. As soon as I was old enough and earning money I would go to see the Cobblers on every possible occasion. The only compensation for being an exile and following an unlikely team (rather than one of the Premier giants – or Division 1 in those days) is that everyone knows you for that connection and asks you about the club whenever they see you.

Following a lower league side also gives you a much better connection to the players. They are prepared to stop and chat and pass the time of day. Back in the 70s, I would always wait to meet the players outside away grounds and Nobby Clarke would get me a complimentary ticket.

My company sponsors a player – Alfie Potter in the 2015/16 season – and we went to do a 'meet and greet' with him in February. I took along my great-nephew Felix, a dyed-in-the-wool Cobblers fan at the age of 12, and he asked Alfie to sign his team photograph. Alfie asked if Felix would like to come into the dressing room with him and get the other players to sign it. Felix was, of course, thrilled. I can't believe that would happen at a Premier League club.

The season 2015/16 has been wonderful, magical, a delight after so many years of dross. No offence to the teams of 1975/6 and 1986/7 – those seasons were particularly enjoyable – but they seem so long ago. On the other hand, the first few games I saw in the sixties sometimes seem like yesterday.

But how does the current team compare with those heroes of 1965/6?

In 2015/16 we have had the arrogance of John-Joe, the solidity of Buchs, the magic of Ricky. We had Adam Smith – so dependable in goal. Concrete Rod. Marc Richards scoring when he likes. A revolving cast on the wing in Lawson D'Ath, Nicky Adams and Lee Martin (for a while). Brendan Moloney coming back after months out with a flawless performance at Coventry and on top of his game ever since.

They gelled together as a perfect team. But the heroes from my childhood *won promotion to the top tier of English football!* It just doesn't seem possible in these days where success in football is so often determined by the size of a club's budget but I was there – I stood at the front of the Hotel End and watched the players come onto the pitch for the last game before we went up (also against Portsmouth). They were carrying banners celebrating their achievement...*our* achievement.

I have no doubt that if the two teams were able to go head to head, the current squad would win by a country mile. Those players of 1965/6 drank, often smoked and the club took no interest in their diet. Training involved little more than kick-abouts and running. Pre-match preparation was a brief chat in the dressing room before the game and then five minutes of running around and half-heartedly kicking a ball about on the pitch. Warming up would effectively be done during the game rather than beforehand. Injuries during play were treated with a sponge dipped in freezing water. That seemed to summarise the extent of every trainer's medical knowledge: there were no physios, sports scientists or rehab coaches. I remember Denis Brown breaking his kneecap in 1967. He had it removed and, when he returned a few months later, played without one. The fashionable injury in those days was 'doing your cartilage'. That would put you out for months.

The team of 65/6 would have been out-run and tactically naive. The current squad would pass rings round them. For all that, I'd back Mike Everitt against Ricky Holmes and Theo Foley against Lawson D'Ath in one on one situations – until they ran out of steam. That is assuming John Kurila hadn't taken our current wingers out of the game by that point. I spoke to John Kurila at the 'Season in the Sun' 50th anniversary reunion. I asked him if he thought he'd ever get to 90 minutes in the current game and, in his dour Scots way, he shrugged his shoulders and said "I'd have to change my game".

Terry Branston against Marc Richards would be an interesting battle. Joe Kiernan v John-Joe in midfield would be fascinating. At the top end of the pitch, it would be good to see Barry Lines taking on Brendon Moloney. But the interest wouldn't last beyond half-time because of the superior fitness, diet and tactics in the modern game. The present team would wear them down and then coast to victory.

Mind you, our current squad would find it difficult to cope with the ruts on the County Ground pitch caused by its role as a car park for the cricket club over the summer months. They have a perfect surface to play on at Sixfields. Using a heavy leather football would also even up the odds – you wouldn't be able to bend *that* like Beckham.

One of my early memories of the County Ground involves the fans changing ends. If the Cobblers kicked towards the Kop in the first half, a swarm of fans from the Hotel End would climb the barrier, walk along the cinder track alongside the pitch to the other end – while the game was in play – and then find a place on the Kop terrace. They would make the return journey at half time. I'm sure the modern fan would find that hard to imagine – or the days before segregation where you'd stand alongside away fans.

I loved the County Ground. I used to walk through the Hotel End on my way from Kingsthorpe to the Grammar School every day, hoping I'd see a player or two. (I never did – but I did get chased by the groundsman from time to time). After the Chester game in 1994 – the first of our two 'Final Matches' – I dug up a small piece of turf and planted it in my garden at home. I hadn't allowed for the fact that it was soon swallowed up by the rest of the grass in the garden and couldn't be distinguished. Nevertheless, a small piece of the County Ground still thrives in Romsey, Hampshire! In 2015 I managed to buy a turnstile from the Hotel End on *eBay*. I had it restored and repainted and it has pride of place in my back garden. It is at times such as these that it is handy to have an understanding wife.

The Boothroyd season of 2003/14 – where we only won 7 games at home and nearly dropped out of the League – had me challenging my loyalty. The Cobblers were in the bottom two from September until just two games before the end of the season – when we won away at Dagenham & Redbridge and then beat Oxford at home. We only survived thanks to Chris Wilder's arrival. I took the view in the spring that I would not renew my season ticket if we were relegated. That was a hard decision to take. But I had to weigh up the 100-odd mile journey from Southampton every week against the delights of playing Bromley or Braintree or Welling United. Thank God we survived and I didn't have to stand by that decision.

Chris Wilder worked wonders with the club. Of the players he inherited, no-one survived to the end of our promotion season. Chris Hackett was the last survivor from the Boothroyd era and he left for Barnet (on loan) in January. Players who could not hack it – yes, Emile, I'm thinking of you – didn't stay long enough to get comfortable.

But Chris so rarely showed us that he was enjoying himself. Was he trying to single-handedly portray the stereotype of the dour Yorkshireman? He must have been thrilled by the 10-game winning streak (not that it was a club record – that was an 11-game run in 1899/1900) but he spent the whole period looking like he was chewing a wasp. Savour it Chris, it happens less frequently than we'd all like.

As supporters of a lower League team, we need the poor seasons – they give us a point on the scale which helps us measure the euphoria of the good ones. And hasn't 2015/16 been a good one – a great one? A season we will all look back on with pride and joy for years and years to come. Thank you, Chris. And thanks to all the players.

They may not have won promotion to the top division like my heroes from the sixties, but to the current young generation they will be heroes for the rest of their lives.

© Martyn Ingram

THE BEST OF TIMES, THE WORST OF TIMES

by Tom Reed

'Don't be fooled by the 'fairy tale' nonsense. Northampton's League 2 title winning season was a nasty affair contrasted by the brilliance of a once-in-a-generation football team.'

The fields are green, the skies are blue, we'll flush ten million down the loo.

I wish I could join in with the happy-clappy 'fairy tale' descriptions of Northampton Town's title winning season. However, the Cobblers' 2015/16 campaign was marred by the potentially criminal 'loss' of a £10.25 million Council loan meant for the Sixfields stadium redevelopment. The only upside of the scandal was the work of a special manager and a talented team who remained united against the odds.

It would be an affront to the suffering and misery experienced by Northampton fans and staff, during the latter end of the Cardoza reign, to suggest otherwise.

How distressing it was to speak to a terminally ill Brian Lomax, father of the supporters' trust movement, who faced death with his life's work unravelling at his beloved football club through the actions of private individuals who should never have got into positions of almost total power.

"Don't accept tin-pot saviours and two-bit conmen believing it's them or oblivion, because it's not," said his daughter Emily in her impassioned speech on the Sixfields pitch as everything fell apart. Fans are still trying to find apt words to describe David Cardoza with the former Cobblers chairman arrested over 'alleged financial irregularities' in January 2016, before being released on bail, in what Detective Chief Inspector Paul Spicer described as a 'very complex investigation'.

As this writer talked with Lomax, shortly before his passing – Brian's voice weakened but his passion for the club still burning bright – I promised I'd do everything possible to promote fan-ownership of Northampton Town going forwards. Swansea City, whom Brian took great pleasure in seeing the Cobblers beat at Wembley in '97, look a good model with their 21.1% fan share retained in their Premier League club after the recent American takeover. Elsewhere, AFC Wimbledon and Portsmouth go from strength to strength with an almost 100% fan stake-holding.

And that brings us back to the pain of yet another financial crisis at the Cobblers: events that seem to happen in a ten year cycle. Yes, there are people directly to blame, some of whom may have their day in court but part of the pain comes from within. How did we let this happen on our watch and how can we stop it happening again?

Did the media do enough early on when there were warning signs to the doomed nature of Cardoza's building projects? What the hell were we doing marching through the streets when the Council (rightly in retrospect) blocked his plans? Why were the likes of Iestyn Pocock shouted down during a Trust meeting when asking pertinent questions over David Cardoza's ever changing plans for a basic football stand?

The response to the 'Save the Cobblers' fundraiser was equally heart-warming and heart-breaking. Seeing loyal fans sell prized possessions and ex-players auction treasured heirlooms barely twenty years after the original trust rattled buckets in Abington Avenue brought a sense of *déjà vu*.

I sat in on supporters' trust meetings this time round when the prospect of a phoenix club – starting way down in non-league a la Hereford – was seriously discussed. I saw Cobblers fans trade blows out of sheer frustration at the thought of losing a proud 118 year history to the 'missing millions' which dwarfed the loot from Hollywood bank heists.

Then there was the real, human tragedy: Brian Lomax passing on with the club in danger; Rob Dunkley, a knowledgeable, loyal and friendly Cobblers fan, who helped out diligently with the 'We Want Answers' campaign, sadly died too, within hours of the 4-3 win at Luton Town and just a couple of weeks after Kelvin Thomas' takeover of the club.

What cut through the gloom, like football floodlights on a cold November night, was the Northampton Town players and staff, the nearest thing to stars in the town for many a moon.

The galactic Ricky Holmes, on another planet to everyone else and gliding along the pitch like some extra-terrestrial. His strike at Luton, one of many goal of the season contenders, brought feelings of sheer elation unlikely to be replicated.

John-Joe O'Toole, the fans' favourite, the black-sheep who found no route for his rogue persona with adoring Cobblers fans and just had to get on with being a decent footballer. O'Toole commanded the midfield in his nonchalant way while supporters sang about his caravan.

These were brilliant times on the pitch, a purity amongst mud-splattered footballers in contrast to the dirty business of supposedly smooth concrete building works.

Don't be fooled by the 'fairy tale' nonsense. Northampton's League 2 title winning season was a nasty affair contrasted by the brilliance of a once-in-a-generation football team.

£10.25 million spent wisely by a progressive club like Burton Albion could represent the verge of Championship level facilities. Instead, the grand sum became a millstone around Northampton's neck in a story which may get worse when the true details come to light. Again, the fight to save the club has been far more impassioned than the fight for justice. It seems these things just happen to little old Cobblers.

Despite having a new chairman who appears to be business savvy, the potential loss of the supporters' trust place on the club board does not fill me with confidence.

In any case, majority club ownership by private individuals has to be called into question, as evidenced by the crises hitting clubs all over the country at the time of writing. Blackpool, Charlton and Leeds are just a few of the teams that show the Cobblers are by no means alone in hitting trouble due to the dysfunctional club ownership model in England.

That brings us back to Brian Lomax, who along with other Cobblers fans set up the first ever supporters' trust at Northampton Town in 1992. It's probably about time we started listening to what they said, albeit decades too late. It might have prevented yet another bust over boom scenario that dogged an otherwise memorable season.

© Tom Reed

THE JOURNEY, NOT THE DESTINATION

by James Heneghan

'While it was a season which ultimately ended in glory, that was only half the story; what really made this season special was the journey, not the destination. Following the dramatic highs and traumatic lows of this remarkable football team only served to reinforce the true definition of what a football club is and what it should really mean.'

Football fans are a curious breed; they spend their entire existence bound to a single club by an unwavering bond, despite being all too aware of the often grim consequences which await them: the crushing disappointments, the unnecessary anguish, the frustration and inevitable heartache, all of which we inflict on ourselves time and again, yet we always go back for more. Non-football folk must watch on with bemusement and curiosity, and wonder why on earth we do it. What possesses us to go back every week, despite knowing the inevitable woe that awaits us?

Of course, there are those fortunate few whose life as a football fan is a constant highlight with success and glory at every turn, but for most, life can often be a struggle, as fans of Northampton Town would testify. Having managed just three English titles in 119 years, success and Northampton are not a natural marriage. With relegations, financial woe and Wembley heartache - and that's just in the last 10 years - those emotions experienced by many football supporters are known all too well to fans of the Cobblers.

Every now and again, though, you're reminded of why you put yourself through the same agonising ordeal week in, week out and why you never once hesitate in showing your loyalty and support season after season. And this remarkable tale, told over nine enthralling months, is the reason behind football fans' obsession with their beloved sport. It's a story that resonated well beyond the boundaries of Northampton, and one which will be remembered and relived through generations, a season for the ages.

For me, it was extra special as this was my very first taste of the Cobblers, assigned to the role of matchday reporter for the Northampton *Chronicle & Echo* barely weeks before the season began. Northampton was not a club I was overly familiar with prior to taking on my new role, especially having lived much closer to several other Football League clubs. A pre-season that offered no hint of what was to come did little to convince me that I had been missing out.

The journey began in mid-July, at Northampton Sileby Rangers, who would provide the setting for both Northampton's opening pre-season friendly and my first Cobblers experience. It was a rather mundane affair - a classic friendly played at walking pace, won by a sole Sam Hoskins strike - and as I watched on from the sidelines, I pondered what lay ahead in my very first season covering this seemingly innocuous club. Not for one minute did I think I would end up hooked by one of the most dramatic, extraordinary and compelling seasons in the club's 119-year history as the all-conquering Cobblers broke records galore in their relentless march towards League One.

It was a stunning rise to the top but, while it was a season which ultimately ended in glory, that was only half the story; what really made this season special was the journey, not the destination. Following the dramatic highs and traumatic lows of this remarkable football team only served to reinforce the true definition of what a football club is and what it should really mean.

A football club is not represented by a badge or a stadium or even a collection of players and people; it is more than all of those things. A football club is a religion that brings people together, it offers hope and inspiration and provides memories that are passed down through generations. Players come and go, as do managers and chairmen, but memories last a lifetime, the sheer unbridled joy at seeing your club achieve something truly special can never be taken away.

For Northampton Town fans, this was their time in the sun. Not a season purely about the glory, this was a season that highlighted all the trials and tribulations of being a football fan, of overcoming the odds to triumph in the most spectacular and unlikely manner. And above all else, what really made Northampton's story so captivating, so compelling, was the fact they gave hope to all other fans of all other clubs who go through the tough times: no matter how bleak things look, there's always hope.

Because while Northampton's story eventually had its happily ever after, it was far from plain sailing.

The season was only a few weeks old when the scale of their financial problems panned into view. Huge debts, winding-up orders, a shocking steel skeleton for a stand. It soon became apparent that the club was on its knees and with seemingly no way out, it left them staring into the abyss. But united as one, fans, players and staff refused to be beaten, rallying around each other like never before to haul themselves out of the mire.

Adversity has claimed many victims but it would not claim Northampton. Many of football's greatest, most heralded teams have triumphed in the face of such adversity but few, if any, have ever undertaken such a tumultuous voyage towards the Promised Land, not just surviving but thriving and using the bad times as a catalyst to achieve something magical.

Every great fairy tale needs a knight in shining armour and Kelvin Thomas was Northampton's as in he swooped to rescue the club with an 11th hour takeover, just days before a second High Court hearing.

On the pitch, the players, backed by their magnificent and unwavering supporters, defied the odds to go on a relentless march up the League Two table, with a stunning run of 17 wins from 20 games between October and February providing the backbone of their title assault. From 10th to eighth to fifth to third and eventually, after a dramatic 4-3 win at Kenilworth Road in December, to the top of the table, all in the space of two months.

Not only were they winning games for fun, they were playing some wonderful, thrilling, glorious attacking football in the process, hitting teams with pace, energy and relentless pressing. It was a joy to watch, made all the more exhilarating given that it had been inspired against the backdrop of the off-field turmoil. There was more to come, too.

There was the stunning 10-match winning run, memorable triumphs at rivals Plymouth, Oxford and Leyton Orient, as well as the 24-game unbeaten run that ultimately saw them over the line. Winning the league so emphatically and so early might give the perception that Northampton simply steamrollered their way to the title, but aside from the occasional thrashing, such as the one at Leyton Orient, it wasn't quite that straightforward. With 20 of their 29 wins coming by just a single goal, the Cobblers were pushed close by many teams in many games throughout the season, but they always had something extra, that invaluable knack to win games of football and defy the odds.

It's not something which can be measured in ability or skill or talent and it's not something that you can bottle up and take with you. It's something which ultimately makes the difference between good players and good teams and the best players and the most successful teams. Northampton had the class but they also had the desire, the work ethic and the sheer refusal not to be beaten to go with it, something which is a necessity if you have any ambitions of becoming the best. This was team who never knew when a cause was lost, overcoming the odds time and again to snatch late wins and turn potential defeats into valuable draws. And there's another reason why this story is such a special one.

What turns a good season into an unforgettable one are the moments which linger, the moments which will forever live in the memory and stir up the emotions whenever they are recalled. They don't necessarily have to be remembered for the right reasons, but one way or another, they act as the lasting images when everything else starts to fade. Sure, Northampton provided plenty of happy memories - from Chris Wilder's speech at Meadow Lane to Ricky Holmes' late stunner against Stevenage - but those were made all the more glorious and joyous by the torture and agony endured by many just a few short months earlier.

One poignant moment in South Wales sticks in my mind. As Northampton's future became increasingly bleak, with huge debts, off-field disputes and takeover delays, the emotions grew more sombre by the week, none more so than at Newport County where Chris Wilder gathered his players for an emotional, prolonged post-match huddle before they headed over to applaud their fans. The club was fighting a winding-up order, Kelvin Thomas' proposed takeover had stalled and the players and loyal staff had just gone unpaid. The end truly did feel nigh. A few tears were shed on that fateful afternoon as fans feared for the future of their club. You can lose your keys, you can lose your job, you can even lose your wife, but you should never lose your football club.

And ultimately, that's why this season stands out above all others - Northampton fans and staff didn't just save their club, they came together to inspire one of the most remarkable rags-to-riches stories ever witnessed. In a world full of so much hate and anger, football needs more stories like Northampton's, proof that the bad guys don't always win and that there's always hope, always another day. After all, that's why we all follow a certain club through thick and thin. It's not just escapism from the realities of life; it's hope, it's joy, it's despair, it's all those emotions rolled into one.

In the future, when someone asks you why you expend so much time, effort and expense to follow a football team, just point them in the direction of Northampton Town. Supporting a club is not meant to be easy, and as the Cobblers proved in 2015/16, it's the low moments which make the good times all the sweeter. Whatever happens in the future, whatever stories are written, Cobblers fans will always have this season to remember, a true footballing fairy tale that will be relived, retold and treasured for decades to come. A season for the ages.

© James Heneghan

IN SEARCH OF OUR DERBY

by Rodney Marshall

'Does Northampton Town enjoy a proper local rivalry, one which matters deeply, both to 'us' *and* to 'them'?'

History books tell us that, in England, football local derbies have been taking place ever since Boxing Day 1860, when Hallam FC played Sheffield FC, in what became known as the 'Rules derby'. [1] In theory, these matches are the most eagerly awaited fixtures, clashes between close neighbours where the ground is packed and where there is a genuine edge and tension, both on the field and off it. Cross-city rivalries are, traditionally, the most intense, and this is certainly still the case in places such as Sheffield and Bristol, or with the North London encounters between Arsenal and Tottenham. Victory in a derby offers one set of fans the perfect opportunity for territorial one-upmanship and online or office bragging rights, despite the all-too-frequent darker underbelly of alcohol-fuelled, tribal violence which accompanies the match day itself.

You don't have to be neighbours to be rivals, of course. Long-standing rivalries can develop between clubs which are hundreds of miles apart. Manchester United v Arsenal matches, for example, took on a more intense flavour during the Ferguson/Keane, Wenger/Vieira years. These games became battle grounds with something of the atmosphere and hostility of a derby match. Lower down the football food-chain, there is the oddly-named 'Dockland derby' between Plymouth and Portsmouth. Despite the distance involved, a 340 mile road trip, the fixture has taken on some of the intensity of a genuine derby match. Nevertheless, for the purpose of this article, what interests me is the concept of the local derby match. Does Northampton Town enjoy a proper local rivalry, one which matters deeply, both to 'us' *and* to 'them'?

Geographical proximity does not guarantee a genuine, mutual sense of rivalry. Neither are these rivalries set in stone. The idea that they are timeless is a myth; as with most aspects of football history and culture, it is far more complicated than that. While tradition is an important element in local derbies, current success — or lack of it — can colour the local football map. This partly explains why Liverpool v Manchester United matches at Anfield are played out in an atmosphere which has, arguably, more tension to it than the traditional Merseyside derby. In Nottingham, while County is the older club, Forest's on-field superiority over a number of decades has led to a situation where many Forest fans view County almost fondly, as a luckless neighbour, and see Derby County as the genuine local rival, the club they love to hate. This rivalry has also been partly fuelled by historical events which have changed the way people 'read' the region's (football) map. During the Miners' Strike of 1984-5, increasing political and ideological tension between Derbyshire and Nottinghamshire people drip-fed into the local football clubs, adding a deeply unpleasant edge to the matches between Derby and Forest and Chesterfield versus Mansfield. The tensions, created (or intensified) by the ripple effects of social conflict, can remain in place long after the event itself. Equally, notions of cultural difference, including national identity, can fuel local rivalry, as in the 'Cross-border derby' between Wrexham and Chester.

Neither is the football map itself a static one. MK Dons is an obvious example of this, one which I will return to shortly. Robert Maxwell's attempts to merge Reading and Oxford – as Thames Valley Royals – in 1983 had a knock-on effect for the aptly-named 'Thames Valley derby'. In addition to controversial mergers, regional boundaries change; new clubs are formed; others go out of business; clubs arrive in, or disappear from, the Football League; some find themselves in an unfamiliar division for an extended period of time…all of these factors affect local rivalries. [2]

I'm in danger of sounding like a sociology or history teacher, so let's cut to the chase and bring in our beloved Northampton Town. Elsewhere in this book, I have described the Cobblers as a 'hub club', one which is geographically situated at the heart of the English footballing map. This freak of nature means that there are, fortunately, a large number of professional clubs within easy driving distance, making each one a potential local rival. The official club website recently highlighted the fact that the majority of next season's League 1 opponents are within a hundred mile radius. In theory, it should be easy to cherry-pick a juicy local derby. However, football is rarely that simple.

For veteran Cobblers fans, Coventry was traditionally an important local derby, although – as with Leicester City – we have barely played each other in recent decades. (Does Coventry's brief tenancy at Sixfields change the dynamics or relationship? Probably not.) For others, the arrival of Peterborough United in the Football League in 1960 created a new number one neighbour, battling it out for the 'Nene derby', or even the 'Northamptonshire derby', as Peterborough was in the county until boundary changes were made. [3] The more recent formation of Rushden and Diamonds added a far more local rivalry, although it was always destined to be a short-lived one. Meanwhile, the arrival of Chris Wilder, Kelvin Thomas and a number of players from Oxford United added colour and tension to a local derby which was previously fairly low-key. Last season's on-going debate (or dispute) about which of the two teams was 'better' – fuelled by the managers themselves, players, fans, journalists, social media and other clubs – has added another layer to the neighbourly banter. Closer to home, the controversial creation of MK Dons has added a further dimension to the local footballing map.

Just who are NTFC's main local rivals, then? One of the problems is that most of the potential candidates are already engaged, as it were, to another club. Oxford have Swindon (the A420 derby); Luton have Watford (the M1 derby); while Peterborough and Cambridge have their cross-county rivalry. Oxford will always view us as a minor distraction compared to Swindon or Reading. [4] Luton's Kenilworth Road is a horribly good ground for Cobblers fans to visit: prehistoric facilities but a crackling atmosphere created in the oddest location for an away end you could find anywhere: the metallic staircases taking supporters over people's back yards before bringing them back down to earth, literally and metaphorically. However, Hatters fans will never consider Northampton as serious local rivals. Coventry tend to look to the Birmingham area for theirs. In League 1 they currently have Walsall close by and the sense that ours is an East versus West (Midlands) battle limits the sense of a genuine derby, even though we are far closer to their city than we are to Peterborough (35 as opposed to 45 miles). Older Posh fans may be happy to renew an intense rivalry, now that we are back in the same division as each other after a fair few years apart. However, the notion of a 'Northamptonshire derby' is outdated, an anachronism, and won't mean anything to younger supporters.

Are there any Posh fans looking out for the Cobblers' matches on their 2016-17 fixture lists? I fear that we probably feature below the likes of Coventry and MK Dons on their radar nowadays. Maybe they are even busy dreaming about promotion back up to the Championship and rediscovering East Anglian battles with Ipswich and Norwich.

From a personal point of view, I have missed the annual Peterborough encounters. Part of this, admittedly, is nostalgia. In the early 1980s – the era which fully formed me as a Cobblers fan – there were few away fans in the old Fourth Division. If the likes of Mansfield, Lincoln or Wimbledon were enjoying a promotion campaign, they would attract a sprinkling of travelling supporters onto the uncovered Spion Kop at the County Ground. However, many clubs brought no one at all, and you could frequently have the away end to yourself if you wanted a left-field view of proceedings, which I occasionally did. However, when Peterborough were in town it added an extra dimension, a proper match-day feel. Not all of this was healthy. There was a tribal edge to the fixture: mounted police, scuffles near Abington Park, etc. Nevertheless, there was also a genuine atmosphere, particularly when the fixture was a festive one and the County Ground would suddenly come alive. The fact that so many of our players were ex-Boro no doubt helped. [5] Times change, though, and many would argue that the Posh/Cobblers rivalry has lost its cutting edge appeal.

Inevitably, all this speculation leads me to conclude that our biggest hope, in terms of establishing a genuine local derby and rivalry, is MK Dons. Geographically, they are closer than anyone else (22 miles). They haven't yet established a proper rivalry of their own, with the obvious exception of the 'Ideological derby' with AFC Wimbledon. [6] I'm not convinced that the 'Buckinghamshire derby' with Wycombe means that much to them. Some of their support comes from places which were – traditionally –

Cobblers territories, in terms of supporter recruitment: Bletchley, Wolverton, etc. Their proposal to build a state-of-the-art training facility near Cosgrove, in an area of natural beauty in South Northamptonshire – which has featured in the local press this spring – has not only raised objections from villagers but also annoyed some Cobblers fans who have complained (on fan forums) that this constitutes encroaching on 'our' area. This kind of dispute over borderlands and territories is, traditionally, exactly what is required to fuel a proper local rivalry. Mix in the army of 7,000 who marched on Stadium MK in January; the (vague) sense of injustice when they overcame us in that replay to earn a plum, televised FA Cup tie against Chelsea; [7] debates about whether MK Dons is a proper club, based on their short but highly controversial history; and a mild sense of envy relating to the fact that they possess what we would love to have – a large, ultra-modern stadium – and you have all the ingredients needed for the perfect pairing. Our club website has described it as our 'geographical derby', but we need something catchier than that. Any suggestions are welcome. In the meantime, Shoe town versus Concrete Cow city, bring it on!

© Rodney Marshall

1. The match was played using the Sheffield Rules, a football code devised for use by Sheffield FC and a major influence on the modern game.
2. Examples include the Bradford 'Wool City' derby between City and Park Avenue, now relegated to that of a potential pre-season friendly; or the emergence of Fleetwood as Blackpool's new local rivals, replacing Preston North End.
3. Peterborough remained geographically part of Northamptonshire until 1965. From 1965 until 1974 it was in a new county called Huntingdon and Peterborough. Since then it has been in Cambridgeshire, although Northamptonshire is called the city's 'Historic County'.
4. Reading, in turn, are seen as the poor relation in the 'Didcot Triangle', despite their greater achievements in recent years.

5. Typically, the starting eleven against Villa in the 1983 FA Cup tie included four ex-Posh players: Heeley, Massey, Freeman, and Syrett.
6. Here, the animosity is mainly one-sided anyway.
7. We were left to regret the misfortune of two deflected Dons goals in the original 2-2 draw and woefully incompetent refereeing decisions in the replay which the MK Dons manager acknowledged post-match.

AFTERWORD: HARNESSING GOODWILL

by Rodney Marshall

'Goodwill – often in short supply – needs to be harnessed, or else it soon evaporates. Diehard supporters have long memories, but floating fans have short ones.'

There is a well-documented dark side to social media and the internet in general, including the insults traded and hatred spread like a disease by 'faceless fans' on many football forums. It is all too easy for people to sit behind keyboards, screens and pseudonyms, typing or texting furiously and thoughtlessly, sending out their comments anonymously. These sites, arguably, need to be moderated with far more sensitivity and intelligence. Nevertheless, as I sat down to start writing this final chapter, it was the positive side to *Twitter*, *Facebook*, etc., which was on my mind. It was a warm Sunday evening, hours after the Champions' open-top bus parade through the gloriously sunny streets of Northampton, generously lined with cheering fans. Thousands were waiting in the market square and the sharing of photos and snippets of film allowed people from anywhere in the world to join in with the celebrations. This magical, communal side of modern technology is rarely explored by the media. Unfortunately.

Conversely, the fact that so many thousands turned out in person to participate in the event in the real world – rather than simply watch it in the virtual one – demonstrates a number of things: community still means a lot to most people; a football club such as NTFC is at the heart of that community; and the future of the Cobblers is a positive one if the current goodwill can be harnessed. More of that later...

I want to go back three months. Midwinter, with the Cobblers top of the table and people beginning to believe that this really could be 'The Year of the Cobbler'. The February away trip to Leyton Orient was a stark reminder to me of how much our cityscapes and football grounds have changed over the last few decades. I hadn't been there for many years and my memories of Brisbane Road and its surroundings were of 'timeless' streets of terraced working-class homes in the traditional East End of London; the ground itself an open, windswept affair with uncovered terraces giving a panoramic outlook onto high-rise blocks and suburban roads. Now the approach is dominated by the Olympic Park, an enormous waste disposal centre and a thriving community sports venture. The rebranded 'Matchroom Stadium' has modern, expensive apartments on all four corners; the ground is now an all-seater affair and there are no views at all. Its facilities are far better, but you sense that you could be almost anywhere. Once the match began, though, you felt that, on one level, nothing had changed. Raw passion, nerves, anticipation and excitement took over, as it always does. The French have an expression which roughly translates as: the more things change, the more things stay the same. Football fans haven't really changed, even if everything else seems to have moved on.

On the pitch, the game highlighted why being a football fan is such a delightfully perverse experience: you simply cannot predict what is going to happen. There had been no hint before the break that we would witness the sort of magic which arrived after it. It had been an instantly forgettable, insipid, goalless first-half in which we created few chances and, at times, simply hung on. We then witnessed our biggest win of the campaign which included exhilarating, fast-flowing football and two potential goals of the season. That evening, as my son and I headed back to Suffolk, we instinctively knew that we were destined to win the league.

Everyone, it seems, is in agreement that an extraordinary season on the field was made all the more remarkable given the off-field circumstances. And yet, paradoxically, many also feel that the doubt and uncertainty provided an extra motivational factor. As takeover talks stalled and stuttered, many of us feared the worst. Surely we would enter administration, we would be docked 15 points, key players would be sold or even given away, and the council would call time on our 'little football club' in this 'big rugby town'. Incredibly, the takeover went ahead, bills were paid, as were staff, and the team's fantastic form continued. The Borough Council stood by the club and we now had a chairman who was a proper football man. The future looked bright. At Northampton Town? Surely something had to go wrong? No, the fairy tale did indeed have a happy ending, surprising and delighting us all, even though the managerial duo, the architects, left the building at the end of the season.

This 2015-16 Cobblers squad impressed on a number of levels. With so many players in the 28-30 year age bracket they drew on their individual experiences of previous promotion and relegation campaigns to create a collective resolve: tackling the away matches with the same determination and mind-set as home fixtures; maintaining a high level of intensity through a pressing game high up the pitch; battling for every ball and allowing the opposition defence little room to relax. Perhaps most impressive of all was the way previous first team regulars accepted extended spells on the bench (or the stands) as the club reinforced in the January transfer window. The signings were a statement of intent from the board and the manager, but it was the players themselves who had to cope with the fierce competition for places. Four centre backs battling for two places, the same in central midfield and six talented attacking wide men jostling for two or three places. Internal conflict could have resulted from this enlarged squad, yet togetherness and patience were the order of the day. This was the first time in my lifetime of supporting the club that a genuine squad was in place at Northampton Town. 'Genuine' in the sense of twenty players good enough to be picked in a first eleven, rather than substitutes and reserves simply making up the numbers.

With the odd exception – such as Wilder's spellbinding tirade at Notts County – post-match interviews are rarely insightful or quote-worthy. However, back in January, after a comfortable win (3-0 versus Barnet), winger Ricky Holmes talked about the need for all the players to have a first class work ethic and for attacking players to consistently track back. His words struck me as defining the squad's mentality:

"I think that should be embedded into any player. You can't have a luxury player out there because you're going to get beaten. It's not just me who does that. I think it's everyone. The gaffer wouldn't play us if we didn't do that. That's first and foremost. You've got to work hard and earn the right to play...We all work for each other." (BBC Radio Northampton, 02/01/2016)

When your main 'flair player' talks like that it suggests that the winning mentality is in place and that the ethos of the group is a healthy, harmonious, hard-working one. Holmes' words impressed me, and stayed with me, every bit as much as Wilder's more dramatic ones from Meadow Lane had.

Team performances arguably dipped after mid-March. Even so, the unbeaten run continued. Rod Liddle's lavish praise in his *Sunday Times* column included reference to how the team could play moderately but still pick up positive results:

'Northampton are obdurate, extremely well organised and experienced; they win games that they should draw and they draw games they should lose.' (*The Sunday Times*, 01/05/2016)

Pre/post-match, players tended to bring up the same explanations for the invincibility. As full back Brendan Moloney put it: "This is such a tight knit group, and we're all fighting for each other. Everyone gets on really well. You need all of those little ingredients to come together." There was no premature backslapping, nor any sense of over-confidence. Rather than guarding a secret magic formula, there was a simple recipe, including the collective 'ingredients' Moloney referred to.

Wilder half-jokingly suggested that any individuals wanting to put themselves before the team or squad should take up table tennis instead. Of course football is a collective sport and an all-for-one spirit is a key element. However, any winning side also needs talented individuals who can make a difference through a moment of creative magic and, in John-Joe O'Toole and Ricky Holmes, the Cobblers were blessed with two such players. It was unsurprising that both were selected for the PFA divisional side, nor that they finished as winner and runner-up respectively in the club's player of the season awards.

O'Toole – a goal scoring central midfielder – had, as Jefferson Lake remarks, been a 'marquee signing' from Bristol Rovers in the summer of 2014, a player who had scored 15 goals in a relegated side. However, he had failed to deliver in his first season at Sixfields. On the transfer list and rarely picked, his days at Northampton seemed numbered. Brought back into the side for a midweek match at Wimbledon near the end of September, he quickly became arguably the team's key individual. A genuine box-to-box player who could do the ugly defensive work but also offered exquisitely cultured touches on the ball with either foot, allied to an instinctive ability to arrive in the opposition box to finish off an attacking move, his long hair and questionable temperament were no doubt part of his charm for Cobblers fans who have always taken to the flawed hero. He is the perfect example of not judging a book by its cover; such elegance, at odds with his unconventional appearance! [1] Even when the team was playing poorly, as was the case in the first half at both Dagenham and Leyton Orient, he stood out as the one man still performing at his usual high standard, surely the mark of a top player. The manager also deserves a pat on the back here as it would have been easy to give up on O'Toole after that first, underwhelming campaign. (Perhaps Wilder felt that he owed it to himself; after all, it was he who had signed him!)

By way of contrast, Ricky Holmes had endeared himself to the management team from the moment he arrived, initially on loan from Portsmouth. His long-term back injury was a blow early on in the new season; conversely, his return before Christmas was like a major new signing. If O'Toole orchestrated the midfield, here was a guy who could run at opponents, slot defence-splitting passes through the eye of a needle and conjure up spectacular goals at crucial moments in key matches: at Luton, Dagenham, Leyton Orient, and most notably Stevenage...A little magician. With Holmes in the starting eleven or coming off the bench, you felt that anything was possible. Having made the step-up from non-league in his early twenties, he seemed to be on a mission to make up for lost time. He had something of the spirit and hunger of those ex-non-league Graham Carr boys of the mid-1980s – Wilcox, McGoldrick, Hill, Gilbert and Morley. While the team itself was attracting sold-out signs to a three-sided Sixfields, here was the player to get bums *off* seats. Like O'Toole, there was also something of the enigmatic maverick about him. The fact that he made the three man short-list for the League 2 player of the season, even though he missed almost half of it, speaks volumes.

Of course there were other jewels in the crown. Marc Richards, the club captain and leading goal scorer, enjoying an Indian summer in his second

119

spell at the club, endeared himself further by refusing to be sold when the financial vultures were hovering; Joel Byrom, whose sweet left foot was deadly accurate from set pieces; Adam Smith, sacked by Leicester City for disciplinary reasons, looked a class above most rival teams' goalkeepers. You always felt confident that he could win a one-on-one battle with a striker. Before the Cobblers hit their long 'purple patch', Smith won a number of points almost single-handedly. His selection as the Football League goalkeeper of the year and in the PFA divisional team suggests that his performances impressed pundits nationwide. Rod McDonald, plucked from non-league football, soon overcame any early season nerves to establish himself as a quality left-sided central defender; when was the last time we had seen one of our back four score with an audacious overhead kick? David Buchanan was Mister Consistent and an ever-present in the left back role. Nicky Adams, one of an impressive array of two footed players at the club, produced a large number of assists in the first half of the season. Brendan Moloney, Ryan Cresswell, Lawson D'Ath, Danny Rose, Sam Hoskins and Zander Diamond all had key roles, while Josh Lelan, and Alfie Potter also played their part. Ryan Clarke never appeared in a league match, yet his form and presence in training kept Smith on his proverbial toes.

Unlike some previous campaigns which had been littered with a mind-boggling number of mediocre loan signings, the 2015-16 season's eight temporary visitors all played a positive part, particularly teenagers Dominic Calvert-Lewin and Darnell Furlong, with special mention also to James Collins and the returning John Marquis. The loanees even weighed in with almost a quarter of the league goals (twenty of the eighty-two) which were scored by the free-flowing Cobblers.

I cannot complete this Afterword, of course, without returning to Chris Wilder, the Football League Manager of the Season. Like Carr, he took over a side at the foot of the League's basement division, gradually signed his own players and brought the various ingredients to the boil. Praised by his skipper as being an inspirational 'motivator', he always insisted that praise – and awards – for the boss was shared with everyone else working at the club; his tough outer-shell had plenty of humility at its core. Who can forget his emotional reaction at Exeter's St James' Park? A very human outpouring and a fitting book-end to his (equally heartfelt) tirade at Meadow Lane. Liddle rightly praised him in his column:

'He is easily the most successful manager so far this season...Wilder has done a remarkable job...be sure to keep an eye on that man.'

Those final words proved to be prophetic, of course, with Wilder making a dream move, just a few days after the final curtain, to the city of his birth, to the club he supported as a child and played for in two separate spells. Sheffield United have signed a wily, determined, intelligent manager who is a fascinating mix of 'old school' principles and modern ideas. It will be a surprise if he fails to inspire one of football's 'sleeping giants'.

The team sometimes looked more at ease away from home. On no fewer than four occasions the Cobblers struck four times in a league match on the road, at Morecambe, Luton, Leyton Orient and Carlisle. We never managed four goals at home. Perhaps the way the team was often set up – 4-2-3-1 – suited a counter-attacking style, with three attacking wide midfielders free to roam across the pitch. Perhaps opponents came to Sixfields and played in a more cautious manner. Certainly, the increasingly large away followings created a carnival, vibrant atmosphere which can rarely be matched at home, where the more vocal fans are liberally spread around. Did this 'away roar' inspire the players? I would certainly like to think so and Wilder frequently referred, proudly, to the modern rarity: a genuine communion between players and fans.

A number of club records were broken or equalled in the League. I highlighted these near the beginning of the book (on page 15) but they are worth displaying again:

- Unbeaten run (24)
- Consecutive wins (10)
- Consecutive away wins (8)
- Away victories (14)
- Unbeaten away run (16)

- Fewest away defeats (2)
- Fewest defeats (5)
- League points (99)
- Manager of the Month awards (3)
- Players selected for the PFA divisional side (3)

That unbeaten run (24) is, of course, still running. Even better, NTFC were *Champions* of League 2, nearly thirty years on from their previous silverware/title, on the back of that incredible league run, a single defeat in thirty-three matches and just two losses in forty; the first League team to be promoted in 2015-16, crowned champions a week later before any other side had even confirmed their promotion...These statistics will never lose their magical appeal. It seems fitting that this 2015-16 squad matched Graham Carr's 1986-87 team in amassing 99 league points. Both sides provided supporters with such a wonderful feast of entertainment, after years of famine.

'The Year of the Cobbler' has been a season with memories we can cherish for many months – and years – to come. The club had previously only won three league titles, if you include winning the Southern League in 1908/09. In other words, it doesn't happen very often, so enjoy the moment! (Unsurprisingly, many of the contributors to this book are keen to point this out.) Besides, you never know what is round the next corner. As with the ongoing development of the East Stand, 'phase one' is complete, and we await the next with anticipation and renewed hope...

This leaves me to close on a note of 'optimistic caution', if that isn't an oxymoron. Throughout my lifetime of supporting the Cobblers, we have taken the occasional step forward, only to then take two back. We have been stuck in a repeating cycle of promotions – creating a series of short-lived false dawns – swiftly followed by relegations. The five promotions since the mid-1970s have seen the club survive in the higher tier for a meagre total of twelve campaigns. We often start brightly in the third tier but, as key players, the manager, or both depart, we shuffle back down to the basement division, as if it is our natural element, where we are most at home. Each time we have come back down, it has felt like an inevitability, as if we were simply out on 'loan' in the rarefied air of higher ground. There has never been a genuine sense of belonging in a higher division, of the club growing and maturing.

Can the instantly likeable and football/business savvy Kelvin Thomas combat this depressing, cyclical structure which seems to make up the Cobblers' DNA and marks out so much of the club's history? Can he rewrite the formulaic script? The swift departure of the Wilder/Knill dream ticket raises all-too-familiar questions and fears for older Cobblers fans who have seen it all before.

Why has our club been stuck in this repeating cycle? After all, Northampton is a large, rapidly-expanding town. [2] The thriving university brings with it a constant flow of young people, many of whom will be interested in football. Unlike clubs such as Accrington, Rochdale, Bury, Oldham, Leyton Orient, Wimbledon etc., we don't have a Premier League giant on our doorstep, whisking potential fans away like the Pied Piper. (It is premature to talk of Leicester City in those terms and anyway – unless you are a crow – our East Midland neighbours are almost forty miles away.) Northampton Saints and the Cobblers are not genuine rivals, competing to attract the same supporters; in general, most people are either fanatic football or rugby followers. [3] Our club is in an ideal geographical location to maximise away numbers at Sixfields, unlike remote or isolated clubs such as Plymouth Argyle or Carlisle United. [4] Housing – for players, managers etc., – is more affordable than in most parts of the South East. We no longer play on a cricket car park which could put off potential signings; instead, we have one of the best playing surfaces in the Football League. There is plenty of room for stadium expansion at Sixfields...The potential is there for all to see; to evolve into a decent Championship club. The support has always, traditionally, arrived when the team delivers. Successive club owners have talked up the 'massive untapped potential' of Northampton Town and other fourth tier managers normally describe the Cobblers as a 'big club' at the basement level.

So what is the problem? There is not a single factor which we can simplistically point to. Northampton Town has never possessed a fan base with the raw passion seen at Portsmouth's Fratton Park. Neither is the football club the sole sporting focal point of the town, unlike in similar size places such as Luton, or significantly smaller ones like Ipswich. Nor is there a rich heritage to draw upon in harder times, unlike at Preston or Blackpool. The club has been guilty, under numerous regimes, of lacking the ambition or vision to press on. Northampton Town has not owned a training ground since the late 1970s, and the current stadium remains a work in progress. The new owners have a number of major hurdles or obstacles to overcome in order to take the club further forward. However, there is no better time to do this than when you already have momentum. 'Consolidation' often means stagnation and it is vital that our club continues to be (realistically) ambitious. While we must celebrate and cherish this historic season, we need to ensure that the adventure merely *begins* here. That is something in which we can all play a role: chairman, the new manager Rob Page, staff, sponsors and us, the supporters. Kelvin Thomas hinted at this unique opportunity in the wake of both the inspired Trophy Tour and what the club called 'Super Saturday', with 3,260 season tickets sold by the (end of May) discount deadline, a 52% increase on sales at the corresponding period in 2015:

'There is a huge buzz around at the moment, the trophy tour with Clarence this week has shown that and there is real excitement around the club and in the community. The whole community feels connected to the club and that has generated a fantastic feel good factor.' [5]

Goodwill – often in short supply – needs to be harnessed, or else it soon evaporates. Diehard supporters have long memories, but floating fans have short ones. Back to Wilder for a final time:

'It's exciting to look forward because the club is on the up…It's really important that we kick-on.' [6]

The 'we' now seems cruelly ironic, yet I couldn't agree more. Let's enjoy the moment, but let's also ensure that this superb, surreal season is the launching pad (for the club we love) to expand: fan base, stadium, structures/facilities, youth academy, local and national profile, corporate sponsorship and ability to attract hungry, passionate, ambitious players... I'm sure you get the picture.

There are also serious questions to be answered about the disappearance of £10 million of public money. Despite the fact that a new regime is in place at Sixfields, the truth needs to emerge and, until that happens, the incomplete East Stand will continue to represent an unacceptably dark stain for many fans and tax payers. A resolution to the mystery of the 'missing millions' will bring about a cathartic release for many of us.

On a brighter note, if that sunny May parade demonstrated one thing, it was that we have, potentially, an enormous Shoe Army! There again, as anyone who experienced and shared both the joy and the misery of those three contrasting Wembley play-off finals will confirm, we knew that anyway.

I was listening to a close season interview with club captain Marc Richards as I finished proof-reading this final piece. He commented, 'If someone wrote a book about this season, you'd never believe it was true.' Well, we have, Marc, and it is. [7]

© Rodney Marshall

1. Liddle described O'Toole as resembling 'an extra from Francis Ford Coppola's *Apocalypse Now.*' Rod Liddle, 'Looking to raise the dead? Send for the lower-league miracle workers', *The Sunday Times*, 01/05/2016.
2. Northampton had an estimated population of 219,000 in 2014. Between 2004 and 2013 the town was in the top ten in the UK in terms of population growth (11.3%). (Source: Centre for Cities' 2015 *Cities Outlook* report.)
3. As journalists such as Graham McKechnie and Jefferson Lake have observed in the past, Saints and Cobblers tend to attract their respective support from contrasting fan bases, social backgrounds etc.

4. Northampton Town, in geographical terms, is a 'hub club'. The official club website announced recently that 14 of next season's 23 league opponents are situated within a hundred miles of Sixfields.
5. Published on the Northampton Town website, 29/05/2016.
6. Chris Wilder cited by the *Chronicle & Echo*, 'Cobblers will not rest on their laurels', 03/05/2016.
7. Marc Richards, NTFC website 31/05/2016.

OUTSIDE THE BUBBLE

by Tom Ingram

'I found myself asking what I would do if it were to fold… Would I feel obliged to support a phoenix club? …Would this be an opportunity to break the connection? How could I fill the vast chasm that the Cobblers folding would leave?'

I hear there is a buzz around the town when the Cobblers are having a good season. I can only assume that this was present again in what proved to be a remarkable year. As an exiled Cobblers fan, growing up away from the town – outside the Cobblers' bubble – I am envious, sad at missing out on the general feeling of excitement.

I like to think that I have a different perspective to that of the average Cobbler, a clarity that can only be attained when looking in from the outside. I was the only kid at my school who didn't support a Premier League team, although I am sure this will be an all too familiar story to many of you. The Football League was a mystery to my friends and the Third Division a standard not worthy of their attention. Yet as a result they were missing out on the true beauty of the game; they didn't experience the same range of emotions, the camaraderie and underdog spirit.

The armchair fans seem amazed by my dedication and the effort I go to following a club who more often than not disappoint. But I have never viewed it as a chore. Missing games always seemed far more difficult to handle than the 200 mile round trip to Sixfields.

I often wonder how vastly different my life would have been if I had chosen my club differently, although in reality it is not something you choose for yourself. Once you experience the vast range of emotions at a football club you know that no other team is capable of making you feel that way.

I was born in Southampton to a Northampton Town supporting father and a Bristolian mother whose family could never quite agree on Rovers or City. As a result, I didn't feel any genuine connection to my local side, but with the bright lights of Premier League football on my doorstep I could have easily found myself following another team. However, watching Southampton almost constantly lose at home in the mid 90's paled into insignificance compared to the exciting drives north to the County Ground, with my father, when the opportunity arose.

My first game in the 1991/92 season was set to the background of an all too familiar cash crisis. However, this was beyond my understanding at the time and it wasn't until years later that I learnt how close it came to being my first and only season following the Cobblers.

Over the next few years I was treated to exciting away trips to Scarborough, Scunthorpe and Shrewsbury. Towns you would never visit if you weren't a football fan. Watching ugly football in dilapidated grounds, amongst a handful of dedicated Cobblers fans, would have turned most children away from the bleak prospect of following the Town. However, amongst those troubled times there was so much to enjoy. The win at Gay Meadow in 93, followed by the infamy of surviving on a technicality the following season, were such major events in the club's history, yet as a child I was almost exempt from the burden of worry. They were exciting times in my eyes, while the context didn't matter.

I was only nine when we played our second 'final game' at the County Ground, so my memories of the ground aren't quite as defined as I would like. I was also never able to witness the main stand in all its glory. I was only once treated to the luxury of the Meccano Stand and even this hastily constructed shell seemed so much more appealing than the stale all-seater football I was treated to elsewhere. I'm not saying that it was always enjoyable. There were nights when the atmosphere was lacking and the games seemed flat, but with the Cobblers there was always a spark.

Despite our troubles, life as a young Cobblers fan seemed like a happy one. As a team, we had plenty of defeats, but as a club we were never defeated. We escaped our financial troubles, we escaped relegation at Shrewsbury, we finished bottom of the Football League and still survived... we seemed indestructible and now we had a brand new home. The future looked so promising.

You live in optimistic hope, waiting for that season where the frustrations pay off and our luck turns. My first taste of this was with our Wembley win in 1997 – this event, as it must have done with many others, condemned me to a life supporting the Cobblers. Once you have experienced such an occasion you know your life will never be the same again. That feeling of ecstasy is something that you always believe is attainable, yet is so infrequent a companion in the life of a lower-league football fan.

This brings me on to this season. A season which has lived up to that ecstasy and gone far beyond. There were so many moments of jubilation that you have to remind yourself from where this amazing run started. This season's financial troubles were a real eye-opener. Having been too young to concern myself with the club's problems in '92, this was the first time that I was fully aware of the club facing the possibility of liquidation. I found myself asking what I would do if it were to fold. I support the club because my father does, and because his father did before him, rather than for geographical convenience. Would I feel obliged to support a phoenix club? Would I feel the same connection with it? More to the point, could I face the 200 mile round trip to watch football in the Combined Counties League?

Would this be an opportunity to break this connection? How could I fill the vast chasm that the Cobblers folding would leave? Perhaps I would find another club closer to home, although I know full well that this would never have felt the same. Thankfully this was not a problem that I had to face and the events of this season have only reaffirmed my love for the club and the sport as a whole.

Everyone knows me as *the* Northampton Town fan, a proud affectation. I know we are dotted around all over, but it is rare to meet another Cobblers supporter outside the county. People have always been keen to talk football with me. They ask lots of questions about life as a fan of a lower league club. However, this season the conversation changed. People didn't want to know about Bayo or our penalty win against

130

Liverpool. People seemed to know about the financial problems; they had read the reports and shared my concerns. They all knew the scores; they had seen John-Joe's goal from the free kick at Luton, Ricky Holmes' volley at Orient and watched Chris Wilder's rousing speech on *YouTube*. They even seemed to know the League Table and permutations. I wasn't able to see any of my friends, my barber, or even the guy at the off-licence without a chat about the Cobblers.

The buzz is definitely spreading and, for once, I don't feel quite so isolated.

© Tom Ingram

THE TALE OF THE COBBLERS' TWIN

by Rodney Marshall

'Absence *can* make the heart grow fonder; a fabulous season also helps.'

2003 found me in a difficult place. I was bored with my job – well, fed up with my career to be more precise – and, more importantly, my personal relationship was breaking up. We'd been together for twenty-eight years, 'a good innings' you might say, particularly in this increasingly fickle world we inhabit. The cracks had been appearing for a long time, but the odd *frisson* of excitement had offered hope, each time cruelly dashed. Another false dawn. Perhaps we had never been ideally suited. We were from different necks of the wood; maybe we simply didn't have enough in common... It was time to shred that season ticket.

Elsewhere in this book, Tom Rostance talks about how – in 2015 – he was in danger of falling out of love with football in general and the Cobblers in particular. I still loved the game; I felt that it was NTFC that was my specific problem. Like a drug addict, I lacked the self-restraint just to stop going to matches. I needed to put some serious distance between us, force myself to move on. The southern half of France seemed like a good idea. A change of climate, change of career, and I could leave the Cobblers to disappoint all the other mugs.

****

When estate agents select properties to show you around in rural France, they have a check list if you are British or Parisian: an attractive view, revealed stone walls, a private garden, enough space for a swimming pool, a barn 'ripe for conversion'... I'm sure you get the idea. The tour of the house is orchestrated to end in the room they feel will sell the place to you. It is their trump card. As a succession of agents showed us around a variety of regions and country houses, I had a trump card of my own. I wasn't going to miss the British weather, food, traffic, or my job as a teacher, but, after nearly thirty years following the Cobblers, there was no way I could survive without my weekly fix of football. As each agent passed me the details for 'the perfect property' and smiled confidently – after all, this was the height of a French property boom – I dropped my bombshell. Of course, a view would be great; yes, I loved the colour of the local stone; indeed, a pool would be a welcome bonus; but I needed to be within an hour of a professional football club. The shocked looks I received were priceless.

You might be wondering why. After all, here in England it would be harder to find a property which *wasn't* located within an hour of a Football League ground. I haven't checked this on *Google Maps*, but I would imagine that you would have to trek into a remote area of, say, Herefordshire or Cornwall to avoid being relatively close to a professional football club. (Land's End to Plymouth Argyle is a good hour and a half's drive.) In France it is very different. To begin with, there are just two fully professional divisions, each consisting of twenty clubs. Even Paris only has two clubs in the top two tiers, PSG and Red Star. Add the fact that France is about five times the size of England and that three of those forty clubs are on the remote island of Corsica — closer to Italy than the French mainland — and you can begin to see the problem. One which had suddenly become a headache for a succession of estate agents hoping to 'close' a deal.

Finding a rural home within easy access of one of those other thirty-five clubs was not as easy as I had imagined. Admittedly, this was partly our fault. We weren't interested in Northern or Eastern France — both hotbeds of football but climatically cold — while South West France tends to be rugby territory. In addition, a fashionable, top-flight club would be no good. It simply wasn't my style. My marriage to the Cobblers might be over, but I quickly realised that I was looking for something similar in my French mistress. Call it old habits and a perverse desire for football delivered with pain and heartache. Anyway, I reassured myself that it would be different this time. There would be the fun of discovering the eccentricities of a new football culture and language. Nevertheless, the search was more complicated than any of us could have foreseen. Many potential properties, and agents, bit the dust. It was then that Lady Luck played her trump card, albeit a wild one.

I struck gold when I discovered an unfashionable region called Poitou-Charentes. Approximately the size of Wales, its capital is Poitiers, which is twinned with Northampton. One of its four departments, the Deux-Sèvres, had a football club, Niort, which played in *Ligue 2* (the equivalent of the Championship). This sleepy town of approximately 50,000 inhabitants is twinned with Wellingborough. It seemed like fate. We viewed a property which we liked and met our potential new neighbour. He told me that Niort had *'une équipe de merde'* (politely translated as 'not a good team') which had spectacularly climbed up the divisions to the very top, only to disappear again after a 'single season in the sun'. The deal was struck. I even loved the club's nickname, Chamois (Mountain Goats), particularly as this is one of the flattest regions of France (think Norfolk or the Fens). [1] This was the club for me… and the house was pleasant too. We ended up living happily in France for a number of years.

****

When I first visited Chamois Niortais' ground, the sense of a connection between my new French club and the Cobblers merely strengthened. I was told that Niort found it difficult to recruit decent players because the stadium was basically an athletics ground; the pitch had a running track around it, reminding me of the old Country Ground, a cricket venue which managed to masquerade as a football stadium for almost a century. They had been actively looking to relocate for a number of years. In vain. It all sounded reassuringly familiar. The Niort club offices were situated in 'Avenue de Wellingborough'. This was perfect. Four season tickets were purchased.

The hard-core support at Niort is housed in a corner of one stand. In this section, it is almost obligatory to carry a flag and to chant throughout the match – encouraged by a man with a loud-hailer who perches precariously on a high metal fence, his back to the action. The rest of the ground remains silent, pausing to groan occasionally. The first season confirmed my long-held suspicions that I am a curse. My arrival as a neo-Niort fan, inevitably, led to the longest-serving second tier club being relegated for the first time in decades. Despite bouncing straight back up as champions the following season, by the time we returned to live in

England successive relegations had seen Niort back in regional football (*CFA*). Even here, in an amateur league, average away journeys are five hours one-way. Thankfully, there are two advantages to regional football: the matches are played on Saturday evenings, while *Ligue 2* games take place on Friday nights, a nightmare for away supporters; also, when you arrive at an away game in the fourth tier the turnstile operators are usually so amazed to see visiting fans that they let you in free of charge. The look you receive is an odd mixture of respect and suspicious incredulity. Normally, the comment that 'we are British' does the trick, confirming that you are, indeed, mad.

There are some genuinely delightful aspects to French lower-division football. When we first arrived, news of an Englishman buying season tickets spread like a forest fire. I became known to everyone as 'Chamois Anglais', roughly the equivalent of 'Frenchie Cobbler'. Fans came up to introduce themselves and offer lifts to away matches. My son and I got to visit the most surreal venues, such as the state-of-the-art Stade Charléty in the heart of Paris. A magnificent 20,000 seater stadium, it is home to the virtually unheard of Paris FC and, on the night we visited, the fifty or so Paris-based Niort fans outnumbered the home support. Each time I have travelled away to a non-league club for a Niort French cup match, victory has seen home supporters lining up to shake our hands on the way out, wishing us luck in the next round. I can't imagine that happening in Basingstoke, Bognor or Boston.

Of course, this being France, bizarre bureaucracy plays its part. The DNCG – an administrative body which polices football – can relegate a club three or more divisions at the drop of a hat and, frequently, fans are left unsure which league their heroes will be playing in until the eve of the new campaign. In *Ligue 2* you get a more thorough search on your way into a ground than you receive at any British airport, even though I've never witnessed any hooliganism. I've arrived at a number of grounds (such as Tours and Laval) where the turnstile staff denied knowing where the away section was, and a handful of us have ended up shuffling around the outside of the entire stadium, periodically asking to be let in. At Metz's impressive ground – a ten hour drive – we were told that there was, indeed, a dedicated away section. However, it might not be opened, as the club hadn't received an e-mail from Niort warning them that there would be visitors. (There were twelve of us that night). On that occasion, we were allowed in, but payback came after Niort scored a stoppage time equaliser and we were locked in for an hour after the match, with the stadium lights turned off. Eventually, a steward turned up with a torch, peered into the inky darkness and – seemingly shocked to discover us – said, *"Vous êtes toujours là?"* ("Are you still there?")

There are other cultural differences, of course. *La buvette* – where you buy your pre-match food and drink – is as important, if not more so, than the match itself. Also, Adebayo Akinfenwa would probably last five minutes on the field of play if he was officiated by a *Ligue 2* referee, as the latter tends to be whistle-happy, card-flourishing and is genuinely insulted by any player daring to make any form of physical contact.

As with every football club, there is a number one fan at Niort, a man whose fidelity knows no bounds. If a family wedding clashes with a pre-season friendly, Stephane Bureta sends the lucky couple a card. Considering the kilometres involved – over land and sea – and the Friday night slot, a season's away trips need to be planned like a Napoleonic campaign and, luckily, his job in a laboratory involves flexible hours, or else he would no doubt have jacked it in. He racked up over 500 consecutive Niort matches at one point, and received a special shirt from the club as a memento. He reminds me of John White at Northampton in the early 1980s, a lovely man who organised the Mounties away travel and lived and breathed the Cobblers, as did his parents. These guys are the lifeblood of any club and make my own passion seem luke-warm.

Naturally, since our return to England, the curse on Niort has been lifted. They have returned to the professional, though still genteel, ranks of *Ligue 2*, where crowds are almost identical to the Sixfields attendances. I loved my years supporting Niort and still watch their matches when I am over there during family holidays. The wonders of the internet enable me to listen to the live commentaries and follow the matches on *Twitter* from East Anglia on a Friday night. If the rural Suffolk broadband was better, I could even watch the action through one of the many illegal live feeds.

I have now returned to the Cobblers fold. Absence *can* make the heart grow fonder and a fabulous season also helps. With hindsight, Niort could never have fully replaced Northampton Town. However, Chamois Niortais was my mistress for a number of years and I couldn't have found a better twin if I had searched for decades. Karim Fradin, their General Manager, even knows about Northampton Town, having played alongside ex-Cobblers winger Ali Gibb when they were both at Stockport County. When I bump into him at pre-season games he usually asks about our previous campaign. Traditionally, I shrug with embarrassment, but I'm looking forward to talking to him this summer.

In the final months of the 2015-16 season, with Niort struggling – successfully as it turned out – against relegation from the second tier, I received lots of messages from fellow Chamois fans, asking me if I could persuade the likes of John-Joe or Ricky to take an extended holiday in Western France. They were all impressed by the goals I had shared from *YouTube*. [2] I told them that the Northampton players couldn't be spared, although judging by the final League 2 table that was a half-truth, at best.

© Rodney Marshall

1. Goat leather was traditionally brought to Niort to make leather gloves, an almost vanished industry which I like to think mirrors Northampton's former shoe trade.
2. Maybe one day we can officially twin the two clubs and organise annual pre-season matches for players and fans. It could be fun.

CONTRIBUTORS

Phil Agius was born in Northampton and grew up in Kingsthorpe before going to Cardiff University. He was a sports reporter for the *Sutton Herald* before becoming sports editor of the *Crawley News* and group sports editor for the *Surrey Mirror* series. He joined the *Racing Post* sports desk in 1999, becoming sports editor in 2007. He lives in Crawley, West Sussex, also obsessing about NFL (Cleveland Browns), Formula One and early 1990s indie guitar bands.

Jeremy Casey was born in Northampton in 1969. He is married (to Fiona) with three children (Ryan, Ewan and Mia) and lives in Abington. He is the sports editor of the *Chronicle & Echo*, and has been since the end of 2005. Prior to that, he spent five years as the Cobblers correspondent for the paper. He has been in sports journalism since the summer of 1987, first for the *Northants Post*. He also covered the Cobblers for that paper for four years. He moved to the *Chronicle & Echo* in 1993, and was a sports writer/ sub-editor until 2000. He has had the pleasure of dealing with and getting to know several Cobblers managers down the years, including Graham Carr and Theo Foley, and then everybody from Ian Atkins through to Rob Page. In terms of all-time favourite Cobblers player, he's going to cheat. Favourite attacker: Trevor Morley. Favourite defender: Ray Warburton. Honourable mention: Ian Sampson. Aside from football, he is a big cricket fan, and loves music, although sadly he can't play a note or hold a tune! He likes all sorts of artists and bands, but his favourites are Paul Weller and The Beatles.

Peter Gleasure is a former Cobblers goalkeeper, the third highest appearance maker for Northampton Town in the club's history. He holds the club record for clean sheets, won a Fourth Division title and was the club's Player of the Season for 1987-88. He is married to Sharon, a health visitor; they have three sons and two grandsons. He runs his own driving school and is a season ticket holder at Luton Town FC.

James Heneghan says that sport has always been by far and away his biggest love; it has dominated his life for as long as he can remember. Having grown up near Hitchin in Bedfordshire, his dad would take him to local games at Stevenage and Luton and that inevitably prompted his desire for a career in sports journalism, especially given that his other passions included golf and cricket. After university, he worked as a sports editor for three years prior to taking on the role of sports reporter at the Northampton *Chronicle & Echo*, just weeks before the start of this amazing story.

Martyn Ingram was born just a few hundred yards from the home of Northampton Town, where his father had a season ticket in the main stand. He moved to the south coast at the age of 12 but continued to follow the Cobblers – going to home and away matches as soon as he was old enough to travel alone. He now drives up from Southampton for every home match with his son, Tom. Martyn works as an Insurance Broker in his own business, *Norris & Fisher*, which sponsors a player each year. His favourite player of all time is Frank Large.

Tom Ingram is an exiled Cobblers fan, born and raised on the South Coast. He is a third generation supporter and season ticket holder, one who follows the Cobblers due to gentle persuasion as well as the threat of being disowned by his father. His favourite player: Andy Woodman.

Jefferson Lake saw his first Northampton Town match from the Hotel End in 1990 but did not truly fall in love with the Cobblers until Morrys Scott's last-minute winner against Barnet in an Auto Windscreens Shield game two years later. In January 2005 he achieved a lifetime ambition of landing the job of covering the club for the *Chronicle & Echo*, a post he held for more than a decade before leaving for *Sky Sports*. His favourite current player is David Buchanan and his favourite player of all time is Kevin Thornton.

Rodney Marshall was born in London but considers Northampton to be his spiritual home. He is a former tutor at Exeter and Plymouth universities and has published books on *The Avengers, Blake's 7, Man in a Suitcase, Travelling Man*, the Nazi war crimes at Oradour and Ian Rankin's *Rebus* novels. He lives in Suffolk. Although he has a football mistress in France (Chamois Niortais FC), he has been married to the Cobblers since 1975. His other wife, Judith, is a Cobblers fan, as is his son, Tomas. (Daughter Jessica prefers animals.) His favourite all-time player is Wakeley Gage, with Steve Massey, Ian Benjamin and Trevor Morley not far behind.

Norman Maycock was born in Duston, grew up in the 50s, and started going up the County Ground in the early 60s. He has 'loved and suffered every minute since'. He wrote the *Abraham Anstruther* column for the WALOC fanzine for many years. He has lived in Chelsea with his

wife for 35 years, but the last time he went to Stamford Bridge was in 1988 when Trevor Morley came to town with Man City in a Division 2 game! His favourite player of all time is 'the wonderful Don Martin'.

Tom Reed is the Cobblers columnist for the *Northampton Herald and Post*. He is the sub-editor of the leading football fanzine STAND and has been published in the *Observer*, *Mundial* magazine and top German football publication *11Freunde*, writing about football supporters' matters. His favourite Cobblers player is Efon Elad.

Tom Rostance is a *BBC Sport* journalist and live text commentator based at Salford Quays. Born in Stafford in 1983, he moved to Northampton just weeks before the title win of 1987. So he is counting both basement league titles in his lifetime as a fan. He once went five years without seeing an away win, was in Darlington on a Tuesday night to see Marc Richards score his first goal for the club and counts Pedj Bojic as his favourite ever player ...maybe Martin Smith...or John-Joe O'Toole.

Joe Townsend is from Leeds. He read Politics at the University of Birmingham, followed by Broadcast Journalism at Birmingham City University. He joined *BBC Radio Northampton* in April 2015.

Gareth Willsher was born on 3rd April 1973 in Northampton and has been Head of Media with Northampton Town Football Club since September 1998. He lives just outside Northampton with his wife Tracy and children Callum and Keira. He has been a Cobblers fan all his life and generally follows all sport, particularly football and cricket.

Printed in Great Britain
by Amazon